Investigations and Progression in
Science

Investigations and Progression in
Science

Robin Smith & Graham Peacock

Hodder & Stoughton

A MEMBER OF THE HODDER HEADLINE GROUP

British Library Cataloguing in Publication Data

A catalogue for this title is available from the British Library.

ISBN 0 340 61903 1

First published 1995
Impression number   10   9   8   7   6   5   4   3   2   1
Year   1999   1998   1997   1996   1995

Typeset by Wearset, Boldon, Tyne and Wear.
Printed in Great Britain for Hodder & Stoughton Educational, a
division of Hodder Headline Plc, 338 Euston Road, London NW1
3BH by Bath Press Ltd, Bath, Avon.

Contents

Introduction

This book is in three sections. The first section describes what constitutes scientific investigations and suggests ways in which teachers can make their pupils progressively more skilful and able to work independently.

The second section of the book gives a series of examples showing how the same scientific theme can be investigated at three levels. The three levels identified are key stage 1, early key stage 2 and later key stage 2. Throughout the text of this book they are referred to as years 1 and 2, years 3 and 4, and years 5 and 6. The differences between investigations at each of these levels are described and help is given in identifying the appropriate science content for each level.

The third section of the book is concerned with how a whole school can plan for progression in science teaching. Practical advice is offered for planning science action plans, running staff meetings and drawing up work schemes.

*Explaining
Investigations and
Progression*

ONE

Are all practical activities investigations?

Not all practical activities are investigations. There are other sorts of practical work which can be done in science. One sort is where pupils are just learning or practising a skill, for example how to use a thermometer or how to record results in a table.

Another sort of practical work is where pupils are actively exploring materials, perhaps provided by the teacher, to give them experience in anticipation of investigations to follow. We often do this by structuring young children's play, setting up interactive displays or taking the class into the local environment. The emphasis in this sort of work is likely to be on observation, which may well be termed 'first hand experience'. It can be regarded as an early stage in scientific investigation, but it is also important in providing the foundation for learning across the curriculum.

A third sort of practical activity is that designed to illustrate a phenomenon, with pupils watching a demonstration or following instructions. There are good reasons for arranging such illustrations, whether led by the teacher or done by children from worksheets. They can give a class shared experiences to discuss and relate to the scientific ideas they are learning, for example, or there may be activities which cannot safely or successfully be investigated by pupils without close supervision.

Often we need to give children tasks which we know they can complete successfully in a lesson. These might lead to investigations, of course, but the practical activities prescribed in many worksheets act as recipes to follow, rather than as a starting point for pupils to begin investigating (figure 1.1).

Take three ice cubes. Wrap one cube in a sheet of newspaper. Wrap one cube in cooking foil. Put one cube on a saucer. Which melts first?

Figure 1.1 A very prescriptive worksheet – how might this be modified to turn it into a starting point for investigation?

What do we mean by investigations?

When children do an investigation, they have to think about specific questions.

What do we want to know?	*Which is the best carrier bag?*
What can we do to find out?	*Put some shopping in each one.*

They may have to rephrase the question so it is in a form which can be tested.

	How much can we carry in each bag before it breaks?

They will probably have some ideas about what will happen.

	Sharp things will tear the paper bag.

Then their tests will have to be planned, and that means more decisions.

What will we change each time?	*We'll test bags made of paper and plastic.*
What will we have to keep the same?	*We must put exactly the same things in each bag, or it won't be a fair test.*
What shall we observe?	*We'll see when the bag starts to tear.*
Can we measure anything?	*Let's weigh the load when it tears.*
How can we record our results?	*Write the weights in a table.*

When they are doing the investigation, they need to keep thinking.

Do we need to do it again to check?	*Let's try another bag of the same sort.*
Is it doing what we expected?	*Look closely – it's stretching.*

After the testing, there is more to think about.

Have we answered the question?	*The bags were different sizes, so it wasn't just a test of what they were made from.*
Could we do a better test?	*Let's get bags that are all the same shape and size to test.*

In summary, these are the characteristic features of investigations:

- Investigations have a purpose – to find out the answer to a specific question.
- The investigators will turn the question into a test, which they then carry out.
- The test is planned so one thing is changed to see the effect(s) it produces.
- Other things which might affect the results are kept the same to make the test fair.
- The effects are carefully observed and, if possible, measured.
- The observations or measurements are recorded.
- The results are used to shed light on the original question.
- The investigation might then be repeated or improved.

Note that investigations are not the only way to find things out in science. It may be more appropriate to do a survey or make lots of observations – this is often true with biological questions, where we cannot control everything. Sometimes we need to refer to books, information technology or people for answers, rather than try to find out everything ourselves.

THREE

What do we mean by progression?

One of our greatest assets as primary teachers is the way pupils explore, ask questions and try to make sense of the world. It may be tiring and challenging at times, but many teachers of young children have built on this curiosity to create an exciting and purposeful science curriculum.

Children's investigations in science can be seen as an extension of their natural curiosity. Their progress can be considered under three headings: the way they tackle questions and challenges; the way they learn skills of investigation; and the way they develop their scientific ideas.

TACKLING QUESTIONS AND CHALLENGES

First, teachers are concerned with the way children approach questions. Do they use their initiative and respond positively when faced with questions and challenges? Our goal is for them to become able and willing to tackle these challenges with less need for adult help. Children should be taking increasing responsibility for their own learning. Progression in this sense is not peculiar to science, although it clearly fits in well with the sort of investigation promoted in science. Science work can support the more general progress we seek in our pupils' learning.

LEARNING SKILLS OF INVESTIGATION

A second aspect of progression concerns the specific skills that pupils need to learn and improve in order to investigate the world. Some of these will be used more in science than elsewhere, for instance:

- handling equipment to help them collect things or to observe more closely;
- making more accurate, quantitative observations;

- planning fairer tests.

Other skills will be applicable across the curriculum, for instance:

- organising themselves and thinking through what they are going to do;
- working collaboratively;
- communicating their ideas in words and pictures.

DEVELOPING SCIENTIFIC IDEAS

A third aspect of progression which is more subject-specific concerns the ideas which pupils use when they seek to answer questions. As they learn about the scientific view of the world, children are increasingly able to draw upon this knowledge to predict and explain. Their investigations should also help them test and extend their understanding. Ideally, their knowledge and their skill at investigating grow together.

Of course, in reality learning is never as tidy as this picture suggests. Learners need to revisit ideas and renew skills. They often seem to stay at one level for a long time. Sometimes they take a step backwards before moving forward again.

FOUR

How do we help pupils make progress?

What we should aim for in our planning is the right combination of challenge and support which will best help a child develop both skills and understanding. The metaphor of a scaffold to support the building of their science learning is appropriate here. So what sort of support should such a scaffold provide at each stage? Let's consider how we might structure a familiar investigation for children at different stages.

At some time, most pupils grow seeds or plants to find out what conditions affect their growth. At the earliest stage, the teacher will provide lots of discussion and direct the task closely. The main aim may be to encourage pupils to offer ideas and questions, or perhaps the emphasis will be on observation. To enable children to focus on testing one key idea, such as what happens if plants don't get enough water, other conditions which might affect their results will be controlled. The first activity in Section 2 illustrates how this could be set up (see page 42 for more details).

For years 1 and 2, teachers might say to the children:

- Do you think these seeds will grow without water?
- Draw the seed and look each day to see if it changes.
- How has it changed?

If children tackle a similar question later in their schooling, they should have more ideas about what might happen and need less direction from the teacher to turn their ideas into a test.

But they will probably need help in planning their investigation and measurement and recording their findings. To make the most of their results, the teacher will have to discuss what happened and their explanations. So, for years 3 and 4, the following questions may be appropriate.

- How much water do they need?
- How can you find out?
- Can you measure anything? Put your results in a table.
- What do your results show?

More advanced pupils will be able to tackle the question for themselves, use their understanding of the other factors that may affect growth, and plan controlled tests to investigate how much a plant should be given. The scaffolding provided at earlier stages has been removed, but further progress needs new challenges and support, often provided by working with peers to tackle more open questions. The group may carry out their own investigation, but continue to use a familiar planning approach and check with their teacher. The following questions might be used with years 5 and 6:

- How do you think each of the things on your list will affect the plants' growth?
- What are you going to measure?
- How many plants will you test?
- Have you made enough measurements to be sure?

FIVE

Whole investigations or separate skills?

Our goal is for a child to be able to carry out whole scientific investigations; with the necessary supporting scaffolding, these investigations can also be the best vehicle for gaining scientific knowledge.

However, it is often appropriate to focus on particular elements of investigation in order to improve children's skills. With a specific focus, the teacher can help the children with a particular skill, for example by showing them how to make appropriate measurements. Skills need to be used in various contexts so children can draw upon them later as they become more independent. We do need to ensure that children are applying the skills since it is often found that, although they have been shown how to do

something in one setting, they do not automatically apply it in others.

We will therefore examine different elements of investigation separately on the following pages:

- observing;
- raising questions, predicting and hypothesising;
- planning;
- doing experiments and tests;
- using results and evidence;
- communication and recording.

However, in practice they are not used in isolation but in the course of an investigation, ideally a whole one which is also concerned with the child's understanding of scientific ideas.

ATTAINMENT TARGET 1 IN THE NATIONAL CURRICULUM

The National Curriculum in England and Wales has identified elements of investigation within Attainment Target 1 (Sc1). Different features have been stressed in successive versions of the National Curriculum, but generally Sc1 has stressed that:

> 'Pupils should develop the intellectual and practical skills which allow them to explore and investigate the world of science.'
> (DES/WO, 1991)

Recent revisions to Sc1 acknowledge that there are many ways of investigating scientific questions

and provide guidance on the issue of whole investigations and the constituent skills that should be taught.

> 'On some occasions, the whole process of investigating an idea should be carried out by pupils themselves.

> 'Pupils should be given opportunities to . . . use focused exploration and investigation to acquire scientific knowledge, understanding and skills.'
> (DFE, 1995)

SIX

Observation

SIMPLE OBSERVATION?

Look at that daffodil, Julie. What do you notice?'

On the face of it, this is a straightforward request which simply requires Julie to observe the flower, but there are a large number of possible responses. These will depend on factors such as Julie's experience or the context of the question. A child at several points in her education might give one of the following replies:

- 'It is yellow.'
- 'It has a trumpet and some petals behind it.'
- 'I can see a long thing in the middle surrounded by five shorter things.'
- 'I think this flower is pollinated by bees because of the position of the nectary at the end of a long, thin tube.'

Each of these observations is true, but there is a substantial difference in sophistication between them. The first three deal with surface features, whilst the fourth concentrates on function.

Observation in science is not simply a case of looking or using our other senses. It means looking with the goal of collecting evidence to help us understand something; the observations therefore need to be relevant to our purpose. Observation is an active process, and the way it is applied depends on the degree of knowledge and understanding which the observer brings to the work.

In the case of the flower, the aspect the child decides to observe will depend on the degree to which the function of the flower as a reproductive organ is understood. For instance, observations may be directed towards seeing how the stamen and stigma are arranged to ensure that pollination takes place. On the other hand, the child may decide to explore the symmetry of the flower or the origin of the flower's scent and nectar.

WHAT TO OBSERVE

Observation is not like taking a shower – the information doesn't just flow over the observer. Instead, he or she has to make choices about what to look for to avoid being simply overwhelmed by the range of possibilities. Take a relatively simple investigation such as exploring the factors which affect the swing of a pendulum. It is possible to observe:

- how fast the pendulum swings;
- how long it continues to swing after being released;
- the distance of each swing;
- if the swing stays in a straight line.

It is impossible for one pupil to make all these observations at the same time, so how does the child decide which element to observe? This will probably be on the basis of previous experience or in response to a suggestion by their teacher, who will need to help children avoid confusion and focus on the relevant observations. If the learner observes without a clear idea of what to look for, it is likely that he or she will flounder.

When scientists make observations they are guided by a theory; only rarely do they make observations without any conceptual framework. As teachers, we should recognise that even young children bring theories to their observations and that this should influence the way in which we ask children to use their senses.

COMPARING AND CONTRASTING

One way to encourage close observation is through comparing and contrasting objects or events. To contrast a daffodil with a hyacinth will probably involve concentrating attention on colour, scent and structure. However, it is important that the similarities between things are also addressed, and children will need more help with this. In the case of the flowers, there are clear similarities in structure and function. Young children will perhaps say that they are both pretty, whilst older children may mention the similarity in the reproductive organs.

At another time of the year, the children may be collecting leaves. Collecting, sorting and recording through pictures can lead to comparing. The need to decide how to group the leaves can stimulate closer observation and discussion. More systematic classification and identification at a later stage requires increasingly detailed observation. These activities should be done with a variety of materials. When studying metals, for instance, other senses could be used to elicit responses such as:

- 'This can feels hard and cold.'
- 'It looks shiny.'
- 'It rings when I tap it.'

USING SEVERAL SENSES AND AIDS TO OBSERVATION

Visual observation can be enhanced by the use of aids such as magnifying glasses and microscopes. The skills in using these needs direct teaching. When using a lens, for instance, many children cast their shadow over the objects they are examining. If the level of magnification of a microscope is too high, it is easy for young children to forget what they are looking for and simply see a random pattern. As with any observation, you have to know what you are looking for before you begin. Binoculars are an excellent adjunct to the winter study of the stars and moon, but children must be warned not to look directly at the sun.

Children should be encouraged to observe with their other senses (touch, hearing, taste and smell), with reminders not to smell or taste unknown substances. The use of all the senses to aid observation means that a greater range of information is available to help the observer understand the world. An unusual material – fresh yeast, for instance – is an excellent starting point for using more than sight. Its smell and texture are, in fact, more significant than its appearance. The skill of observing the texture or feel of a material is often begun with the feely bags common in infant classrooms; but how do we develop this later in children's schooling? One way is through activities such as grading paper or sandpaper by its roughness, or identifying surfaces.

HELPING PUPILS WITH SPECIAL NEEDS

The use of a variety of senses may help children who have learning difficulties, as well as those whose vision or hearing is impaired. Further support can be given to partially sighted pupils by providing large, bright materials. Give them magnifiers and other aids, where appropriate, to help observation. Suggestions on adapting activities for pupils with special needs are given in *Curriculum Guidance 10 – Teaching Science to Pupils with Special Educational Needs* published by NCC.

OBSERVING A SEQUENCE OF EVENTS OR CHANGES

Children need opportunities to observe change. This may be over a short period of time, for example when food colouring is dropped into water. Their observations of changes which take longer, such as the growth of plants, may be improved by drawings and other records of what they see at different stages. Compressing these changes by artificial means can often be quite dramatic. For instance, in early spring, if four chestnut twigs are brought into the warmth of a room on four separate days through the week, they come into early leaf and flower one after the other. The children can then make a dramatic series of observations which would, if done separately, have far less impact.

HOW CAN WE IMPROVE PUPILS' OBSERVATION SKILLS?

Teachers can use several strategies to develop children's observation skills. For example, when taking pupils outside, they can prepare the children for the visit – arrange for them to have initial familiarisation and then closer, structured observation. They can focus the pupils' attention, for instance, by limiting the field of vision through a hoop on the ground or a viewing frame. Inside the classroom, they may arrange displays and events where the children have to look or listen closely.

However, the most powerful strategy is questioning. The type of question that teachers ask children can strongly affect the subsequent observation. If the teacher's question is open, it is likely to cause the child to observe a wider range of things than if the question is narrowly focused. For instance, if the teacher asks the children, 'What do you notice about the moon this evening?', the children's observations are likely to be wide ranging. These might include such things as the moon's position, its position relative to previous evenings, its brightness or the amount of cloud cover. On the other hand, if the teacher wants the children to observe the phases of the moon, a much narrower question, such as 'How much of the moon can you see tonight?', would be more appropriate. Narrow questions can direct observation away from distractions. For example, if children dipping a rock suspended from a spring balance into a bowl of water are paying more attention to the bubbles coming from the rock than the reading on the spring balance, it might be appropriate to ask a more narrowly focused question, drawing attention to the loss of weight rather than the bubbles. Of course,

the teacher may wish to return to the bubbles later.

Pupils can be encouraged to draw up their own list of questions to structure their observations. It they see a purpose, children are more likely to observe with enthusiasm and care. The ideal purpose is, of course, the interest or question which primary school pupils sometimes bring into the class. We can add to this by asking them to share their thoughts through discussion, display, drawing, making a tape, taking a photograph, making a model or appropriate writing.

WHAT DO PUPILS DO AS THEY GET BETTER AT OBSERVATIONS?

- They make more relevant, detailed observations using appropriate senses.

- They repeat and check their observations.

- They make use of instruments to help them observe in greater detail.

- They seek to quantify and measure what they are observing.
- They look for patterns as they interpret the observations.
- They use their observations to raise further questions and hypotheses to test.

SEVEN

Raising questions, predicting and hypothesising

Young children usually ask lots of questions. Although this can prove wearing to parents and teachers, they should be encouraged to go on asking better questions. Indeed, our real difficulties arise when children do not ask questions, perhaps because of the lack of response from adults.

WHAT CAN WE DO TO FOSTER QUESTIONING IN SCHOOL?

- Incorporate questions into classroom displays.
- Collect unusual things to stimulate curiosity.
- Use changes to prompt children to look again and question what they see.
- Start topics with discussions and lists of 'What we want to find out about . . . ? (figure 1.2).
- Play games such as 'twenty questions'.
- Keep a question box or board where children are encouraged to post their own questions at any time.

- Brainstorm questions as a class, accepting any topic at first.
- Encourage all pupils to volunteer ideas and respond to your questions. Reinforce responses by accepting them, praising them and providing time for thinking before they answer.
- Be prepared to answer spontaneous questions from pupils if you can; admit when you don't know the answer and indicate how to find out.
- Set up situations where pupils ask each other questions and learn to accept comments.

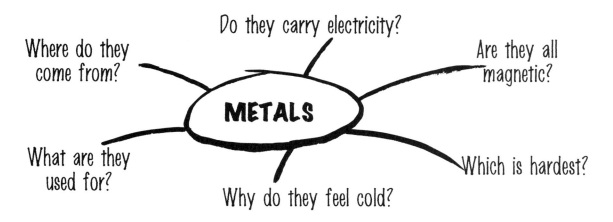

Figure 1.2 What we want to find out about . . . metals

WHY DO WE WANT CHILDREN TO ASK QUESTIONS IN SCIENCE?

In science a questioning attitude is important. We want the school science curriculum to foster this spirit of inquiry. This is worth remembering when there seems so much content in the curriculum.

The National Curriculum emphasises that: 'Pupils should be given opportunities to ask questions such as 'How?', 'Why?', 'What will happen if . . . ?'.

Learning to ask good questions is an essential ingredient for science, as scientific investigations spring from questions and ideas which can be tested. Formulating a good question is often very hard, and planning a successful test depends on a clear statement of the question or problem (figure 1.3).

Figure 1.3   First, clarify what you are trying to find out!

Children's questions also give us insights into their understanding; they can thus help us assess pupils and match our teaching to their needs.

Sometimes a pupil's question reveals that they are thinking about the task quite differently from us (figure 1.4).

Figure 1.4   Children don't always approach tasks from the same angle

WHAT SORT OF QUESTIONS DO CHILDREN ASK?

Children ask questions for a variety of reasons. Some questions are really comments or statements: 'We found some last time, didn't we?'

Young children in particular are likely to raise questions which, to adults, may seem unrelated to the task in hand: 'Can we paint a picture now?'

Sometimes the questions are about opinions or values: 'Do you think it's right to keep animals in cages?'

Many questions can be answered with information from secondary sources: 'How far away is the sun?'

The most productive questions for science learning are those which can be answered by an observation or investigation: 'Why are these plants growing bigger than the ones over there by the tree?', 'How can we stop our ice lolly from melting until we're ready to eat it?', 'What will happen if we use a thicker elastic band?'

WHAT IS A PRODUCTIVE, TESTABLE QUESTION?

A productive question is one that leads to scientific activity, in which the children can get answers through first hand investigation of materials or events. This sort of question is also often referred to as a 'testable', since it can be turned into a test. This is not to deny the value of other ways of finding answers but rather to stress the need to identify those questions which can be answered through investigation. Turning questions into a form in which they can be tested by children requires skill. At an early stage in their science learning, we need to do this for children; but then as they progress, we can help them do it themselves.

Making a question testable means more than simply ensuring it refers to things or happenings which can be studied at first hand. It has to be phrased in a way that allows us to do a controlled test which should yield an answer. This means identifying what we want to change and what we plan to observe or measure as a result. This is examined closely in the section on Planning (see page 17).

Often, our first question turns out to need refining when we have done some preliminary observations or tests. This will certainly be the case where children have simply asked the first question out of curiosity and proceeded to test, 'just to see what happens'. However, when posing a question to investigate, we often already have an answer in mind. This may be expressed as a prediction or a hypothesis.

PREDICTIONS AND HYPOTHESES

The simplest form of prediction children make is when they just say what they expect to happen. We want children to predict, partly to help them plan and think about what they are going to do in an investigation, but also because it encourages them to begin to draw deliberately upon their knowledge. When they have to think about what may happen, they can be asked to consider why – what previous experiences lead them to expect that?

Teachers have to tread carefully here. We need to avoid making prediction into a routine chore ('Do we have to write about it afterwards?' might be replaced by 'Do we have to predict first?' from children eager to get on with the investigation). We also have to beware of expecting young children to make reasoned predictions based on organised scientific understanding. As they progress, however, we should be leading pupils to base their questions and the results they expect upon their growing scientific knowledge, and to become increasingly able to explain this. In doing so, their predictions become more and more like scientific hypotheses.

A hypothesis is an attempt to explain or predict some observation or happening in terms of a concept or scientific principle. Furthermore, in science, hypotheses are expressed in a way that allows them to be tested, and perhaps disproved or supported by the results of an investigation.

HOW CAN WE IMPROVE PUPILS' QUESTIONING SKILLS?

There are several strategies which can be used with a class to develop these skills. One is to discuss how they might go about answering different sorts of questions. Some teachers find it helps to group the questions and get pupils to think about what sort of question they are dealing with.

support them in other aspects of their investigation and concentrate on improving questions and evaluating them afterwards.

Another way teachers can foster pupils' skills is by example; in this case, by modelling good questions in discussion and on worksheets. Listen to their questions and your own carefully. Practise

| To answer these, we'll look in books. | To answer these, we'll do a survey. | To answer these, we'll plan a test. |

If they can identify testable questions, children will still need help in rephrasing them so they can be investigated. Before they plan investigations, get children to talk over or write down their own questions, draft questions in groups, or talk with the teacher individually if they lack confidence. Pupils can also be asked to amend written questions and complete partly framed questions. Refer to their questions as they plan investigations and reinforce this during their tests by inquiring, 'What was it you were trying to find out?' If questioning is the focus of the lesson,

your own questioning skills so you can turn their questions into productive ones. As children get more skilful, ask more from them. For example, in class sessions, gradually make your own questions more demanding. Move from simple recall towards higher order questions requiring pupils to weigh up alternatives.

Useful suggestions on how to improve questioning in science lessons can be found in articles by Eltgeest and Jelly in *Primary Science: Taking the Plunge* by Harlen.

WHAT DO PUPILS DO AS THEY GET BETTER AT QUESTIONING?

- They pause to think about what question it is they are trying to answer.
- They amend their questions so they can be tested in an investigation.
- They seek to base the question on previous

observations and experiences.
- Their questions draw upon their growing scientific understanding.
- They offer tentative explanations in the form of testable hypotheses.

EIGHT

Planning

The first step in planning an investigation – posing a suitable question – has already been discussed. This may be provided or refined by the teacher, who anticipates how the question can be tackled so children can proceed successfully with the task. Children have to learn to think ahead themselves, and this is the starting point for more systematic planning. Look, for instance, at the stages in planning a test to assess toilet paper.

Which is the best toilet tissue?

We wanted to know if these toilet papers really are the best, as the advertisers claim. So our group is going to find out which soaks up most water before it tears.

We have three different sorts of toilet paper. We are going to hold a piece of each across a jar and drop water on them.

We will use a dropper and count the drops. We need to make a table to write the numbers in. We have to get three jars, a dropper and a jug of water.

The drops should all be the same size to make it fair. And we have to drop them from the same height and on the same place.

We will stop dropping when the paper starts to tear. I thought we could stop when the paper lets water through. Maybe that will be the same.

Our teacher asked us how many times we were going to test each sort of paper. We decided three would be enough and then we could use the middle number from each paper to compare them.

WHY DO CHILDREN HAVE TO PLAN THEIR INVESTIGATIONS?

- Plans help children focus their attention.
- Trial and error may shed light on a question, but it is inefficient, and crucial evidence may be missed.
- It is frustrating to finish a test and realise that you don't have all the results you need to answer your question, but that you have made lots of measurements that are irrelevant.

- We want pupils to plan so they get more from their practical activity.
- We also want them to learn how to plan science investigations better and to understand what planning involves. They will need to be taught these procedures.

Teaching children to plan in science is an aspect of helping children take increasing responsibility for their own learning, which in turn allows them to become more independent.

WHEN SHOULD THEY PLAN?

It is worth noting that planning occurs during investigations as well as beforehand. This is especially true for young children, whose thinking is closely tied to their activity. However, older pupils and scientists also make decisions, adjust plans and think ahead as they tackle problems. As teachers, much of our planning is done mentally in the light of experience and pupils' responses, rather than written down before. Pupils should be encouraged to comment on their activity as they carry out an investigation, to try it out and then plan improvements, to discuss it afterwards and suggest how they might have been better prepared. But the main focus on planning should be before they embark on the practical activity. This requires children to pause and make decisions about what they will do, what alternatives to consider, and how to make the most of the investigation that follows.

Although we want pupils to learn to give time to the planning stage of an investigation, a few words of caution are needed here. Children will become frustrated if they have very little time for practical testing because they have to produce lengthy plans; the production of a plan, particularly a written one, could become a ritual, done for the teacher rather than as a real aid to answering their own questions. Pupils may also find it difficult to plan a strategy for a whole investigation and need to break it into parts as they tackle it.

WHAT STEPS ARE THERE IN PLANNING?

- The first step is to decide exactly what they are trying to find out: defining the problem and getting the question suitably phrased ('We are going to find out which ball bounces best. We'll see how high each one bounces when we drop it').
- This is closely linked to the second step, which is to sort out what they will change and what they will keep the same. The things which may vary in any investigation are known as the variables (these are analysed in more detail later). Fair testing involves controlling the ones they don't want to investigate so they can look at the effect of one thing at a time. Children may need to try things out in order to identify variables which could affect their results ('If we drop the balls onto the floor from the same height, we can watch how high each one bounces. But when we tried it, we found the classroom floor is uneven, so that affects how high the balls bounce').
- As well as sorting out which variable they will alter and which they will keep the same, children should think about what they expect to happen. Predictions will depend on previous knowledge ('Samina thinks the sponge ball will bounce highest because it's squashy. I think the hard one will, because golf balls go a long way').
- They should decide what they are going to

observe or measure. They need to get the necessary equipment organised, including recording materials, whether it is paper and pencil, a prepared chart or a computer program. If they work in a group, they may decide on sharing out the tasks ('It's hard to measure how high they bounce, so we are going to stick a piece of paper up and mark it with different coloured pens for each ball. Samina will drop the ball, and I'll stand with a pen where I think it will bounce. We'll swap round and try it a few times. After we've done it, we'll measure the highest bounce for each ball').

VARIABLES

Variables is the term used to refer to things which can change or vary in an investigation. The jargon associated with variables is sometimes confusing. The important thing to be aware of is that children need to identify and handle variables with increasing skill rather than use the jargon themselves. Ideally, they should be able to change just one thing (the independent variable) to produce a change in something else (the dependent variable). These two things are the key variables. Other things which might affect the changes should be identified and, as far as possible, kept the same (the variables to be controlled). This is the basis of a 'fair test', and many primary pupils are aware of the desirability of making tests as fair as possible. Other features of variables can affect how difficult an investigation is for pupils. For instance, how they can be measured (on a scale or simply counted or compared) or if the variables interact and cannot easily be separated.

USING PLANNING SHEETS AND BOARDS

If it is difficult for pupils to plan ahead, and there are a lot of things to consider, so we need to provide support. One well-tried way of doing this is by using a standard format to structure their plans. If they become familiar with a format, they can use it regularly, becoming more independent and organised as a result. Of course, the teacher will not only need to show them how to use it but also ensure they see the value of it in their subsequent investigations. There are many versions of such formats, which can be presented as worksheets, on boards, or even on a word processor. Children can write in the blanks as they plan, write cards or 'post-its' to stick to a board, or get someone to note things down as they talk about their plan. The detail and structure of any planning sheet can be amended to match pupils' progress. Figures 1.5 and 1.6 show two examples which might help children at different stages.

OUR PLAN   Names:

This is what we want to find out.

Here is a picture of the things we will use.

This is what we will do.

Figure 1.5   Planning sheet for infants

HOW CAN WE IMPROVE PUPILS' PLANNING?

Give young pupils a lot of support: plan with them, talk about what they could do and help to organise their tests. With older pupils, discuss their plans with them before they begin. Ask them to redraft their plans after discussion with you or with one another in groups. Encourage them to refer to their plans as they do tests, amending them if necessary. Use problems which could have been foreseen as opportunities to discuss planning. After their tests, ask them to evaluate plans. Compare how well different groups' plans worked out.

Be careful, however, not to allow children to get frustrated by failure or feel they are being criticised unreasonably. Don't emphasise planning so much that it seems more important than the investigation. After all, the point of planning is to help us do something more successfully.

PLANNING YOUR TESTS	
Talk about these things	Write what you decide here
What is your question?	
What will you change to answer it?	
What do you think will happen?	
What will you keep the same so it is fair?	
What equipment will you need?	
Do you need to draw a table to put your measurements in?	

Figure 1.6 Planning sheet for juniors

WHAT DO PUPILS DO AS THEY GET BETTER AT PLANNING?

- They look before they leap – giving time and thought to how they are going to carry out the test.
- They consider the key variables in their planned investigation.
- They seek to control other variables and plan fairer tests.
- They design their tests so they are likely to answer the question they posed.
- They plan the whole investigation and organise themselves before starting.
- They evaluate their plans, think of improvements and try them out if possible.

NINE

Carrying out tests and experiments

Practical activity will be the most visible feature of children's investigations. Indeed, it is desirable to see pupils using materials and equipment during science lessons for many reasons:

- children are motivated by the practical aspects and enjoy using equipment;
- much of their learning occurs through direct experience and exploration of materials;
- skills are learnt and reinforced through their use in practical tasks;
- ideas can be tried and information gained at first hand;
- the practical activity provides the real test of their hypotheses and plans.

BEING ORGANISED AND SETTING OUT TO COLLECT EVIDENCE

Young children's play contains the seeds of investigation and has its own purposes. We want children to continue to enjoy their hands-on exploration of the world but to be able to investigate effectively as well. To do this, they need to be organised and systematic. Above all, they need to focus their attention on the purpose of the activity and to collect evidence which will shed light on the question being investigated. In the early stages, teachers will have to provide much of the organisation for children and oversee activities so they can collect relevant evidence and stay on task. As they progress, pupils should be expected to take increasing responsibility for organising themselves and carrying out their tests, as in the following example from Section 2 (see page 103) where children investigate how sounds travel through tubes and string telephones.

String telephones can be investigated with pupils of all ages. Infants will need help to use them and to compare the different ones you have prepared. Around years 3 and 4, begin with only one key variable to change – for example contrasting types of string, ranging from fine dental floss to thick wool – and keep other things, such as the distance and the containers, constant. The task for years 5 and 6 can be left open, to challenge able pupils, or more guidance can be given. For example, you can help them to identify and list the variables to control and test one at a time (for instance, shape and size of container, how the string is connected).

These are the sort of things which teachers might say to children.

1 2 Questions and ideas	Tests, observations & measurements	Evidence and explanations
Do you think you will hear me through this tube? Will you hear me if I whisper?	What else could we use to listen through? Which is best for hearing really quiet sounds?	Which worked best? Why do you think it was this one?

3 4 Questions and ideas	Tests, observations & measurements	Evidence and explanations
Which string do you think will make the best telephone? Why? Does it have to be tight to work?	How will you test your idea? How will you decide which string is best?	What did you find out? Why do you think that string worked best? What else might you change on the telephone?

5 6 Questions and ideas	Tests, observations & measurements	Evidence and explanations
Have you made string telephones before? What things do you think affect how well they work? Make a list.	Which thing on your list are you testing first? What other things do you have to keep the same? How many tests will you need to do?	Put your results in a table and write a report to explain what you found out.

PROGRESSION IN TASKS

The demands of tasks need to be matched to the pupils' abilities, ideally providing not only the scaffolding for successful completion but also the stimulus for them to move up a step. Here are some features which can be adjusted to make tests more or less demanding.

- The physical skills required: can the children manipulate the equipment (for example, bulb holders) or is it designed for those with finer control? Have they learnt how to use the tools correctly and safely (for example, wire strippers and screwdrivers)?
- The familiarity of materials and equipment: pupils are likely to find it easier to work with everyday materials, familiar contexts (for example, investigating dissolving with drinks,

changes of state with foodstuffs) and with equipment that they have seen before, rather than specialised apparatus.
- Language: the style of writing and specialist terms often used in science may make simple tasks more difficult for pupils (for example, 'Suspend the load from a newton force meter. Find how much water it displaces when immersed').
- Maths: the language and units used to refer to size or number, including numbers involved in measurements and the quantities which children have to conserve and measure (for example, 'The volume of the water displaced was 1350 ml').
- The co-ordination of many bits of equipment, paper and potential messy materials; working

independently or collaboratively; getting practical activities done in time and tidying up!

- Recording results while carrying out the test and observing; having to attend to more than one thing and remembering to make regular observations.
- The difficulty of the ideas and the complexity of the variables. We have already looked at variables (see page 19). The difficulty of a task is affected by the number of variables pupils have to consider, by whether they might interact with one another (for example, washing powder tests may be complicated if some powders work better in warm water, others in cold and if they also vary according to the sort of dirt being removed). If children can say how things vary simply by categorising them (for example, grouping flowers by colours) or counting them (for example, the number of petals), this will be less demanding than if they need to measure them on a scale (for example, the height of the plant).

TEACHING CHILDREN TO MEASURE

We should make pupils aware of the value of measurement and teach them to measure with increasing accuracy during their investigations. However, this needs to go hand in hand with their learning of mathematics, and we should not expect young pupils to make sophisticated measurements. They have to progress from comparison through non-standard units to standard measurements and then learn to use more specialised measuring instruments, for instance thermometers or spring balances.

Robust measuring equipment with clear simple scales is needed in the early years. Ensure children understand how to use it and get plenty of practice at the skill in tasks where the objective is clear, such as comparing their own vital statistics, checking the amount of water to give their plants, weighing the ingredients when they try different scone recipes and timing one another in races.

What should pupils measure in science?	What equipment do they need?
Children should learn to measure length, weight, volume, time and temperature regularly to gather evidence in investigations.	Rulers, metre rules, tapes; stopclocks, stopwatches, timers; measuring jugs and containers; sturdy thermometers covering the right range of temperature; weights, scales and balances.
They should be introduced to other measurements, such as force, and begin to apply them, for example, in testing friction.	Spring balances, force meters, digital electronic scales.
They may have opportunities to measure sound or light, and to log temperature with computers.	Sound and light meters; sensors and software and computer interfaces.
They should be able to draw on their mathematical knowledge to measure quantities such as area or angles where appropriate, for example, investigating reflection.	Protractors, clinometers.

Some children may have difficulty measuring because of their poorly developed skills, or a specific problem with sight or perhaps co-ordination. Simple adaptations can help; for instance, adding food colouring to water to make it more visible, making sure equipment is at a level where pupils in wheelchairs can see it, supporting measuring equipment so it is stable. There are instruments and low-vision aids designed to help partially sighted pupils.

CHECKING AND REPEATING

As they get older, children need to be encouraged to check their observations and measurements. Eventually, this should lead them to recognise the need to repeat measurements to make their tests more reliable. They may need reminding and helping to organise this. Charts or databases might be useful when there is a lot of data to record during an investigation.

USING INFORMATION TECHNOLOGY DURING INVESTIGATIONS

As well as using wordprocessors, databases or spreadsheets, children may employ IT in other ways during their practical activities. Sensors which measure and record data on the computer can be a valuable extension of some investigations. For example, temperature sensors are helpful if children are testing how different insulating materials slow the rate at which water cools in containers. The sensors and software record the temperatures, display them and allow pupils to trace the changes rather than devote all their efforts to trying to read the thermometers in time. There are sensors for light and sound and others that can be adapted for keeping weather records.

However, in many situations it is better for children to use less sophisticated equipment, for instance when the task requires them to observe directly or practise measurement skills. Sensors and other aspects of IT should be seen by teachers and pupils as a tool to use when appropriate to enhance investigations. Further guidance on using IT in science is provided in books by Frost, Johnsey and the NCET (see Bibliography for details).

HOW CAN WE IMPROVE PUPILS' INVESTIGATIVE SKILLS?

There are many ways in which teachers can improve pupils' skills at carrying out tests and experiments. They can teach skills such as the use of measuring equipment and reinforce them in more than one context. Tasks can be structured so there are not too many or too few new challenges. Teachers can show children how to get organised before they start, check their plans and refer them to their plan during the investigation to keep them focused. During the activity, they can supervise and intervene if necessary to keep them on task, prevent frustration, and remind pupils of the need to measure where appropriate. After investigations, they can praise and point out what pupils have done well, and help them evaluate their performance. In the longer term, they can provide time for extended investigation or opportunities when children can develop their own ideas.

WHAT DO PUPILS DO AS THEY GET BETTER AT CARRYING OUT INVESTIGATIONS?

- They organise their materials and themselves with less direction from the teacher.
- They control variables and check that their tests are fair.
- They make increasingly accurate measurements.

- They repeat observations or measurements.
- They work systematically to collect evidence relevant to their original question.
- They record measurements or observations as they make them.

TEN

Using results and evidence

The purpose of investigations is to collect evidence which answers a question or makes sense of something. So it is important that pupils use their results rather than simply accumulate findings. Recording and explaining results should help children and should not be simply a routine or a chore: 'Miss, do we *have* to write about it after?'

COMMUNICATION

Communicating ideas and findings is an important feature of science. In school, it is also crucial for effective learning. In early proposals for the science National Curriculum in England and Wales, communication and groupwork were given extended treatment. Scientific activities provide pupils with vehicles for extending cross-curricular skills in language and collaborative group work. These in turn enable children to carry out more effective investigations. They extend their scientific understanding by having to express ideas and hear others comment on them.

In science lessons, therefore, pupils should talk and share their thoughts with partners, in small groups, as a class and with their teacher. As their skills with language and mathematics increase, children can use other ways to communicate. There should be a purpose and an audience for this. In time, they should realise that exchanging and commenting on findings is an important aspect of scientific activity.

RECORDING RESULTS

Is it always necessary to record results? Not always, but it is usually worth making a record of some sort. Sometimes the most fruitful use of the limited time for science in school is to concentrate on the activity and discussion. This is especially true with young children, but older pupils may also find over emphasis on producing a record frustrating or fail to see the point of it.

Children and teachers sometimes wonder whether the point is really to please someone else – the children have to show some product to their teacher, who in turn has to be able to show the head, parents or inspectors that work has been done. There are some arguments for recording science work to demonstrate or assess what has been achieved. However, here we are more concerned with reasons which directly relate to the activity in hand and which enhance learning through investigation. There are several such reasons:

- Observations or measurements need to be recorded accurately at the time so they can be referred to later.
- Making a record can focus and improve observation.

- There are skills (such as using tables) which can be learnt and applied by recording results.
- Results can be checked, repeated and critically examined to improve the design and conduct of investigations. This can only be done if there is some record to inspect.
- Pupils need records of their results so they can analyse and interpret the evidence.

WHEN SHOULD PUPILS RECORD?

Traditionally, experiments are written up afterwards. However, there are often things to record during and sometimes before an investigation. In some investigations, it is essential to note initial measurements and observations before starting. ('We should have written down how long the elastic was before we stretched it!').

When children are measuring or observing changes, there can be much to record during their tests. This may be hard for them to organise or to maintain when they are concentrating on the task. Teachers have to decide whether to give

them support, for example in the form of charts or worksheets to complete. More advanced pupils may be able to plan how they will record.

There are some tests in which records need only be made infrequently, and we have to ensure children are not waiting unproductively, for instance when water is cooling slowly in insulated containers. Observations of plants, the weather and the moon are examples where the time scale is so extended that the challenge may be to ensure pupils do not forget to make them or become bored.

HOW CAN PUPILS RECORD?

- Direct records (for example, displays of their model bridges with the loads they carried, or their parachutes hung in order of effectiveness).
- Tape recording (for example, of noise carried through different insulating materials).
- Pictures (see page 29).
- Tables (see page 32).
- Graphs and charts (see page 32).
- Writing (see page 33).
- Use of IT (for example, concept keyboards, word processors, desktop publishing, databases, spreadsheets).

This list summarises a range of ways in which records might be made in lessons. It does not include other equally valuable methods children can use to communicate their findings and ideas beyond the lessons (for instance, through drama or song, presentation in assembly, demonstration to parents or displays for the school).

During their schooling, pupils should be introduced to a wide range of recording methods. In the early years, their teacher will often direct their recording closely. Displays of the pictures and short pieces of writing which children produce may be used as a learning resource.

Later, pupils can produce more precise accounts and graphs, but they will still need lots of guidance on how best to present their results. Eventually, the goal is for children to use appropriate methods chosen from their repertoire, but they will only be able to do that as a result of cumulative teaching over the years and discussion of the choices available to them.

PICTURES

A good picture may well be worth a thousand words in recording and presenting information. However, it takes skill and practice to make pictures accurate, relevant and clear so they convey the essential information. Pictures should certainly not just be seen as an easy alternative to writing or only for use by younger and less able pupils; although pictorial recording is of course particularly appropriate for young children, and certainly their pictures can be vivid records of what they saw and did. Over the years, pupils have to learn how to use pictures effectively and, in time, to adopt conventions for showing essential details and for recording diagrammatically.

Observational drawing is a strength in many primary schools, and pupils can be taught to look closely by focusing their attention on details. For their scientific recording, they will also need to identify relevant details and to show them in their drawing.

Pictures can be used in many ways. Drawings are powerful for showing contrasts, comparing similarities and differences, for recording grouping and sorting activities (figure 1.7). Sometimes it is helpful to make a sketch for later use, especially when outdoors, for example to help identify a plant back in class (figure 1.8). Drawings can also be a quick way to convey an idea or summarise equipment (figure 1.9).

Remember, however, that pictorial recording is

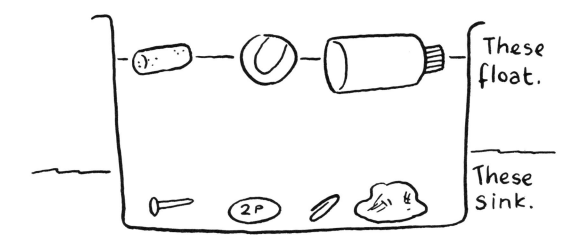

Figure 1.7   Drawings can be used to show contrasts

this flower Was White, it had five Petals, the Leaves Were in threes, it was small.

Figure 1.8   Drawing flowers and plants outside can serve as a reminder when back in class

We tested how strong Magnets were.

Figure 1.9   Drawings are a quick way of summarising results

not restricted to drawing. Other media can be used to convey colour, which is sometimes important but not always easy to capture, for instance the colours of a candle flame or the changes as leaves decay. Large-scale pictures and collage can be useful to apply scientific ideas or to bring together work by several children. Imaginative pictures can, for instance, be used to create habitats based on investigations of environmental factors.

To record events, changes and sequences, children can use zig-zag books, cartoon strips, or three-dimensional representations (for example, of food chains). For older pupils, a series of pictures is an effective way of recording a procedure, such as separating mixtures by filtering and dissolving (figure 1.10).

Figure 1.10   Recording events, changes and sequences

TABLES

Tables are particularly helpful for organising and keeping track of information and can be used before, during and after investigations. Teachers can provide them ready made, if children need lots of support, or they can suggest a format or prompt more advanced pupils to draw up their own.

As they get better at using tables, children will be able to use more rows and columns. Children need to be taught to extract information from tables and to look for patterns or surprises in tabular results. They have to learn how to turn information from tables into graphs. Computers can help them record and use the information; spreadsheets allow children to enter their data directly onto the computer.

GRAPHS AND CHARTS

Pupils will make increasing use of graphs and charts as they collect more measurements. They help to summarise and present results, show patterns and relationships between variables. However, drawing graphs should not become too time consuming or laborious.

At the earliest stage, children can make direct graphs with objects they used (for instance, 'these are the things we piled up to break each bridge', 'here are the pieces of elastic we stretched'). They can then use simple ways of representing quantities (such as pictograms and symbols) and measurements (such as cutting and sticking down strips of card to show the heights of growing plants).

At the next stage, children can make simple charts or block graphs for discrete data and later progress to line graphs and scatter graphs which show relationships. They need regular reminders about drawing axes and scales.

In their book *Making Sense of Primary Science Investigations*, Goldsworthy and Feasey offer further guidance on progression in the use of graphs, charts and tables.

IT can also be useful if the program allows pupils to try different ways of showing the same data and produce a polished product. Computers can construct graphs from data entered onto spreadsheets. Even the simplest spreadsheet packages include programs such as Graph-IT, in which children are prompted to enter single pieces of information to produce graphs. There are also more flexible programs, such as Eureka, which are harder to use. This was used to draw the table in figure 1.11 and then to turn the same data into the graph in figure 1.12.

	A	**B**
2	120	55
3	104	50
4	107	52
5	119	61
6	121	62
7	103	55
8	110	55
9	152	67
10	132	61
11	103	52
12	112	53
13	119	54
14	106	47
15	98	44
16	121	63

Figure 1.11 Computer programs such as Eureka can produce tables ...

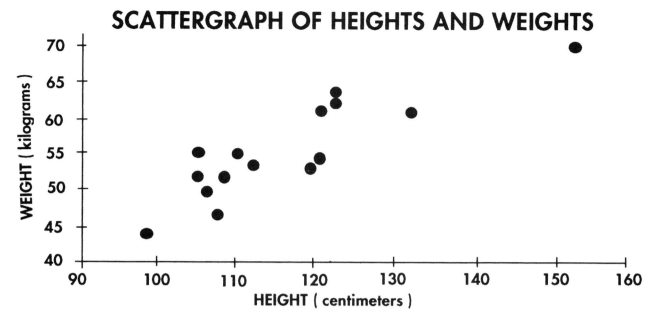

Figure 1.12 ... and graphs of results

WRITING

Where necessary, talk can be taped or transcribed. Scientific activities can be a stimulus to write, but we have to beware of turning them all into writing tasks. There are many sorts of writing which pupils can employ in science, for example:

- notes taken to record key events;
- short descriptions of observations;
- summaries of what they did during the investigation;
- accounts of results;
- summaries of findings;
- more extended pieces presenting their ideas and explanations;
- whole structured reports, perhaps using a standard format.

Writing in science should not be seen as a dry and impersonal experience. There are times when a

more personal piece of writing is in order to express the child's views and feelings, or a creative piece which fosters understanding and enjoyment of scientific ideas.

Some children may need particular help because of language difficulties or specific disabilities, and alternative modes of recording might make it easier for them to concentrate on the scientific aspects of the task. There are several alternative ways in which such pupils may be helped to record: for example, direct recording and display, sorting and sequencing pictures, tape recording and photography, and producing large, textured charts. For some pupils, symbol systems can be a substitute for writing.

Use of the word processor and concept keyboard can also support less accomplished writers. Word processing can thus enhance writing in science. If children draft and discuss their work, this leads to a more precise account, and the word processor or desktop publishing set-up can help them produce a polished report.

Often the audience for children's writing will be the teacher or other adults, but children should also read and interpret accounts by one another.

INTERPRETING RESULTS

To make the most of the investigation, the results need to be interpreted and evaluated. There are several reasons for children to devote some of the limited time available for science to examining and discussing their findings.

Looking for patterns

Seeing regularities in observations or measurements is one of the keys to understanding what was going on in an investigation. In the early stages, teachers can help by stressing recurring events and repeated associations ('There always seem to be lots of snails in the school garden after we water it') which could lead to predictions ('To make the snails move in the plastic box we could use the plant spray').

If things are being compared or measured very simply, they can be ordered or ranked ('Here are the paper aeroplanes we made. This sort usually flew furthest. Then this sort. These were the worst fliers'). As they get older, children can be helped to make sense of their measurements by taking the middle value (the median) or by calculating the mean. We can also help them to lay out their tables and graphs so patterns are more evident, and to search actively for regularities and relationships ('How far did the cotton reel go when you wound the elastic ten times?', 'What happened when you wound it twenty times?', 'Is there a pattern in the way everyone's pulse changed?').

Referring to their original question

Many investigations begin with a question, and the results should help children answer it. At first, young pupils may be quite convinced that their investigation has done this, whatever the evidence, and be content with having done their test. Quite often, it will only provide a partial answer, and older pupils should be asked to consider what else they need to do ('So have you found out which colour shows up best? Can you say which colour bike riders should wear for safety?', 'Do your results tell you which cloth to use for a winter coat? Or do you want to find out any more about the cloths?').

Evaluating, improving or having new ideas

As pupils examine the results and talk about how they did the test, its strengths and weaknesses should be brought out. With prompting, children will extend their appreciation of controlled and repeated tests (in other words, of reliability). They will also begin to appreciate the need for careful planning if investigations are to test what they should (that is, to be valid).

HOW TO IMPROVE PUPILS' SKILLS IN USING RESULTS

- Show children a range of methods for recording results. Teach them how to use pictures and words appropriately for communicating in science.
- Provide support when they use new recording skills, if that is the aim of the session. If the focus is on some other aspect of investigating, do not make the recording too difficult.

- Display and discuss the children's work in order to highlight good points.
- Employ IT where it can help pupils handle results.
- Don't forget that the recording and interpretation of results is done to help answer a question or make sense of some phenomena, not for its own sake.

WHAT CHILDREN DO AS THEY GET BETTER AT RECORDING RESULTS

Children's progress in recording results in science will, of course, be closely related to their language and mathematical development. Their drawn or written product may not accurately reflect their ability to investigate. To assess pupils' progress at recording and using the results of their investigations, we can look for evidence that they:

- focus on relevant details;
- give clearer, more accurate accounts of observation;
- record numbers and measurements accurately;

- handle data in a more systematic way;
- use a growing range of recording methods and begin to choose suitable methods;
- seek patterns and identify relationships in their results;
- evaluate their results and those reported by others.

Above all, we hope children will apply what they learn about recording to help them investigate more effectively and independently.

Investigations and Ideas: Examples of progression

This section of the book is designed to help teachers carry out investigations at the appropriate level with their class. It contains thirty-three double-page spreads. These are grouped around themes which are listed below.

Growth
Seeds and seedlings
Plant growth and change

Small animals
Favourite food
Habitats

Weather
Weather patterns
Wind

Materials
Powders
Absorbency
Evaporation
Washday
Candles
Temperature change
Bouncing balls

Air resistance
Parachutes
Light objects
Gyrocopters

Floating and sinking
Why things float
Displacement
Upthrust
Boats

Electricity
Batteries and bulbs
Conductors and insulators

Magnetism
Magnetic strength
Compasses

Light
Sight
Light sources
Shadows
Reflections

Sound
Sound production
Sound insulation
How sound travels

Earth in space
The sun's apparent movement
A model globe

The left-hand page in each double-page spread outlines activities for pupils in infant (years 1 to 2), lower junior (years 3 to 4) and upper juniors (years 5 to 6). This is indicated by the year number at the side of the activity. The right-hand page of the spread is divided into three parts:

- guidance on carrying out the scientific activities with the three age groups;
- things teachers might say to help children with their investigations (these are grouped under three headings to highlight important aspects of investigation);
- selected points of scientific information shown in the boxed area.

ELEVEN

Using the pages for progression

Each theme is divided into activities and questions suitable for infant (years 1 to 2), lower junior (years 3 to 4) and upper junior (years 5 to 6).

PROGRESSION IN A CLASS

A teacher working with one age group will be able to follow the activities for that group of children from page to page (figure 2.1). For instance, a teacher of a year 3 class might follow the middle section of suggestions for work on how we see things followed by work on light sources and reflections. However, he or she might also look at the earlier infant sections for preparatory investigations and also dip into the related upper junior work for more able pupils.

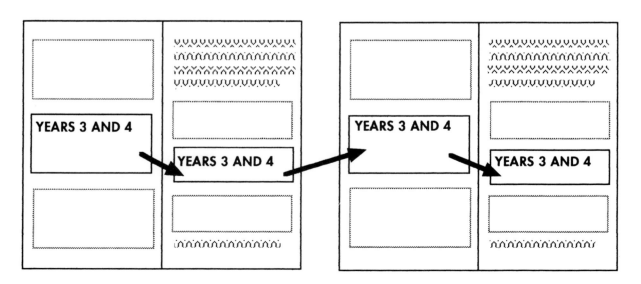

YEARS 3 AND 4

YEARS 3 AND 4

YEARS 3 AND 4

YEARS 3 AND 4

Figure 2.1

PROGRESSION THROUGH THE SCHOOL

A teacher with responsibility for co-ordinating science in the school will be able to look at the development of investigations on any one theme throughout the school (figure 2.2). The idea of displacement, for instance, could be tracked from early experiences of floating through to investigations with boats for older children. The different approaches suggested for each age informs the work of all the teachers in the school, helping them to become more aware of progression and continuity.

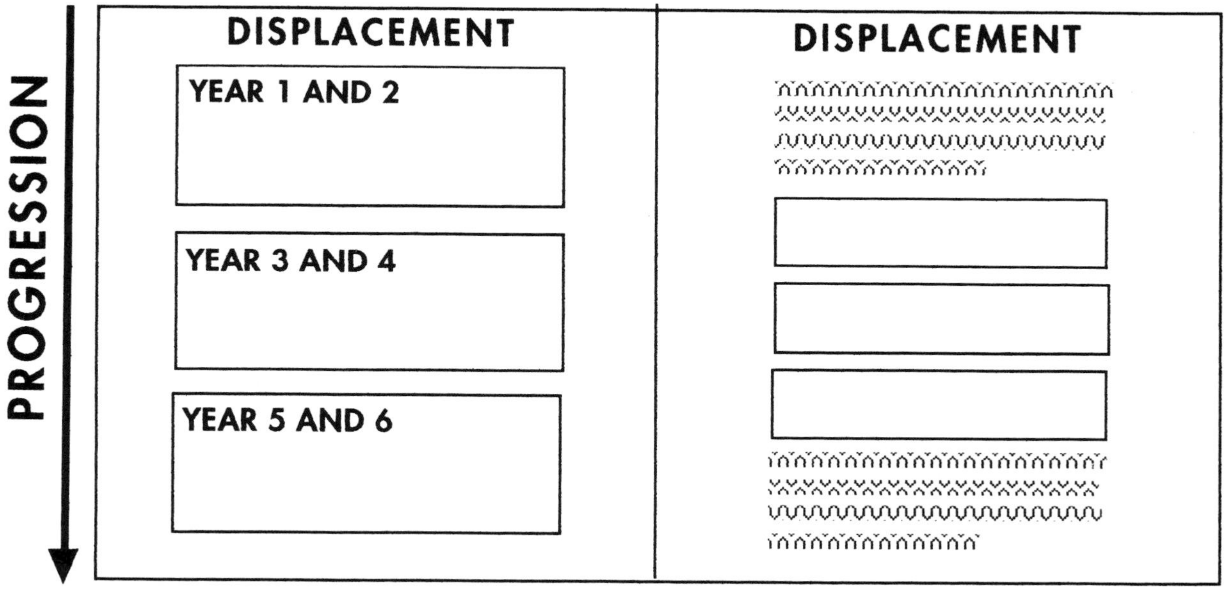

Figure 2.2

Y1–Y2

Will all these seeds grow?

We are keeping these seeds dry.

We are keeping these seeds damp.

We are keeping these seeds very wet.

Y3–Y4

How much water does a plant need to grow? Plan a test to find out.

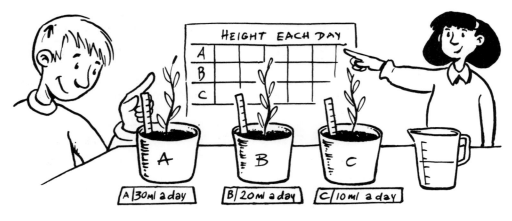

HEIGHT EACH DAY

A
B
C

A 30ml a day

B 20ml a day

C 10ml a day

Y5–Y6

What things do you think affect how well seedlings grow? Make a list. Plan tests to find out how much they affect growth?

Will they grow in the fridge?

LIGHT ALL THE TIME

DAYLIGHT

SHADED

INVESTIGATING SEEDS AND SEEDLINGS

Pupils in years 1 and 2 should look after plants and discuss what is needed to make them grow. Focus their attention on one condition; water is the easiest to investigate. Keep the others, such as temperature and light levels, the same. They should learn to record results as they water and check growth regularly. By years 3 and 4, children should have ideas about how water will affect growth and be able to plan tests of their predictions. They could use runner beans they have germinated previously in big pots or bedding plants from a garden centre planted into trays of potting compost. Help them decide how much water to give and what to measure, for example, number of leaves, length of stem.

Remind them to record their measurements regularly. By years 5 and 6, pupils show know of several influences on growth from previous work on plants. They should discuss which they can investigate themselves and then design an investigation of one at a time, for example light, keeping others, such as water, the same. Asking pupils to plan and carry out the whole investigation could be a challenge to help the teacher assess their learning or it may be directed by the teacher to teach a class how to plan, using a planning chart or board (see page 19). The following boxes suggest things teachers might say to children.

1 2 Questions and ideas	**Tests, observations & measurements**	**Evidence and explanations**
Do you think these seeds will grow without water? Do you think they need lots of water?	How much water shall we put in this one? How much in that one? Draw the seed and look each day to see if it changes.	What happened to your seed? How has it changed? What happened to the dry seeds? What happened to the wet ones?
3 4 Questions and ideas	**Tests, observations & measurements**	**Evidence and explanations**
What do you think would happen to these plants if we didn't water them? How much water do they need? How can you find out?	How much water are you going to add to this pot? How often will you water? How can you record any changes in the plants? Put your results in a table.	What happened to the plants in each pot? What do your results show? Have you found out how much water these plants need?
5 6 Questions and ideas	**Tests, observations & measurements**	**Evidence and explanations**
How do think each of the things on your list will affect the plants' growth? Which could you test (e.g. light)?	What are you going to measure (e.g. light levels)? What do you think will happen to the plants? How many plants will you test?	How did changing the amount of light affect the growth of these plants? Have you recorded enough measurements to be sure?

KEY INFORMATION FOR TEACHERS

Seeds and seedlings need warmth and water to grow. Seeds will not normally sprout if they are cold, dry or waterlogged. Plants need enough light to grow, but seeds can sprout without it. The amount of light can be measured with a light meter or sensor. The effects of low light levels may be more complex than pupils expect and prompt further investigation, for instance into the tall, thin, pale plant grown in low light.

Y1–Y2
Draw the bulb. Look at it each day to see if it changes.

Y3–Y4
Look closely at the buds. Draw one and take it to bits to see what is inside. Stand a twig in water. Make a diary to show how it grows.

Y5–Y6
How fast does the grass grow? What do you think will make grass grow faster? Grow some grass in trays to find out.

INVESTIGATING PLANT GROWTH AND CHANGE

In years 1 and 2, children should grow plants and care for them. In spring, they can observe changes outdoors and investigate them indoors. Bulbs are useful for this, as they can be grown in pots. The changes from bulb to tall, flowering plant can be recorded directly by moving the plant along each day and marking its height to produce a simple graph. By years 3 and 4, pupils should be expected to record relevant details in drawings and use measurement to investigate changes, for example the length of leaves and their appearance as they unfold. The teacher can cut a few twigs with secateurs and chop some buds lengthways with a sharp knife. Paper copies of leaves can be used to record their increasing area directly, while more advanced pupils might measure total leaf area in standard units. Relate their indoor observations to seasonal changes in local trees. The spring growth of grass provides an opportunity for pupils in years 5 and 6 to do more controlled investigations on a small scale, using turf or grass seed and multipurpose compost from a garden centre. They could measure average height or longest piece, or cut sections and measure the increasing weight of grass. Once they have a satisfactory way of measuring growth, they can plan investigations of their hypotheses about how growth is stimulated, for example by warmth, rain and fertiliser (N.B. lawn feed can be used, but not the sort with added weed killer). The following boxes suggest things teachers might say to children.

1 2 Questions and ideas	Tests, observations & measurements	Evidence and explanations
What parts can you see on this bulb? How will it change as it grows?	What has grown bigger? How tall is it today? What else has changed? Draw a picture of the bulb.	Use your drawings to tell the story of how the flower grew out of the bulb.
3 4 Questions and ideas	Tests, observations & measurements	Evidence and explanations
What can you find in the bud? Which bits of the buds will grow into leaves? Which will become flowers?	How big is the unfolded leaf? How much has it grown? How else has it changed?	Did all the buds open out in the same way? Did some grow faster than others? Which grew biggest?
5 6 Questions and ideas	Tests, observations & measurements	Evidence and explanations
The grass is growing now it is spring. What do you think causes that? Plan a test to see if you are right. How fast do you think it grows?	How can you measure how fast grass grows? How often will you measure it? Will you be able to cut some to help?	Can you use a graph to show how fast the grass grew? Does your method of measuring work well? Is it accurate enough?

KEY INFORMATION FOR TEACHERS

Spring growth from bulbs and buds and dormant plants can be rapid when enough warmth and water and light become available. As well as getting bigger, they change shape. Growth of grass is affected by the soil (for example, how well it drains, the nitrogen levels, the acidity) and by people cutting, rolling and walking on it, as well as by rain and light and temperature.

Y1–Y2

Do snails eat lettuce?

Y3–Y4

How could you find out the favourite food of these snails?

Y5–Y6

In a garden with many hungry slugs, what plants would a sensible gardener grow? Design a test to see which plants slugs avoid and which they eat most.

INVESTIGATING FAVOURITE FOOD

Keep the snails and slugs in a plastic aquarium covered with a lightly weighted lid. There is no need for any breathing holes in the lid. Put a layer of damp soil or sand in the bottom of the aquarium and keep the atmosphere in the tank moist, otherwise the animals will be inactive. Snails will readily eat coloured card, and their droppings indicate their colour preference. Ask the children whether a card lid is a good idea. In the example for years 3 and 4, the children may try putting the snails in a darkened tank to see if

they still go to their favourite food. They may suggest trying to hide the food behind barriers to stop them seeing the food. The children in years 5 and 6 may suggest things like carefully drawing the leaves so they can compare them before and after being nibbled. Gardeners sometimes say that slugs will attack plants which have already been damaged. The children could add this test to their slug investigation. The following boxes suggest things teachers might say to children.

1 2 Questions and ideas	Tests, observations & measurements	Evidence and explanations
Do you think all the snails will eat the lettuce leaf? Where do you think the snail's mouth is?	What other food do you think the snails will like? Do you think they will eat coloured card?	The snails' droppings have turned pink. Why do you think that has happened?
3 4 Questions and ideas	Tests, observations & measurements	Evidence and explanations
How many foods do you think it would be sensible to test at one time? How long do you think we should leave the food in the tank?	Where will you start the snails in your test? Are they facing one of the foods? Is one of the foods closer than the others?	Do you think the snail can smell its favourite food, or does it find it through seeing? What clues have you got from your test?
5 6 Questions and ideas	Tests, observations & measurements	Evidence and explanations
Design a short questionnaire to ask people with gardens what sort of plants slugs eat and what sort of plants they avoid. Use the results to plan your test.	How will you know which leaves the slugs have eaten during the night? How will you know if only part of the leaf has gone?	Do you think you would get the same results if you left the leaves you have tested in a garden? What might be different there?

KEY INFORMATION FOR TEACHERS

Snails and slugs are both molluscs. The slug has lost the shell still retained by the snail. They are both gastropods (they walk on their stomach). Their mouthparts are equipped with a rasping radula which wears away food. They do prefer partly decayed plants, and whilst they are not exclusively vegetarian, they prefer plants. They will avoid very

tough leaves, like holly and laurel, and those with chemical defences, like pine. Both slugs and snails have two pairs of antennae; the top set has rudimentary eyes, whilst the bottom set feel and smell the environment. Both types of animal have breathing holes on the sides near the front. These open periodically.

Y1–Y2
Where can we find tiny animals in this wild area?

Y3–Y4
In what sort of places do you find most earthworms?

Y5–Y6
Do you think there are more tiny animals living in long grass than in short, well-mown grass?

INVESTIGATING HABITATS

You can find a great many tiny animals in places where they can get shelter and food. Places such as under stones, in rotting wood and in long, damp vegetation provide both. The best containers to use for collecting small animals are either shallow plastic dishes with lids (petri dish) or any plastic container with lid. The activity for years 3 and 4 will involve the use of trowels. The test can be made fair if the same amount of soil is removed in each place. Try using an old washing-up bowl for this purpose. Provide disposable plastic gloves if you are concerned about dirty hands or possible contamination from dog or cat droppings. Children in years 5 and 6 should be able to select from a range of sampling methods, such as using hoops or string lines to define small study areas. Get them to design their own recording sheets and methods of search. The following boxes suggest things teachers might say to children.

1 2 Questions and ideas	Tests, observations & measurements	Evidence and explanations
Do you think we will find many tiny animals in the playground? Why do you think that? Where would be good to look?	Count how many tiny animals you can find in each place. Remember to put them back afterwards.	Where is the best place to find tiny animals? Which place has no animals?
3 4 Questions and ideas	**Tests, observations & measurements**	**Evidence and explanations**
Which place do you think will have most worms? How could we compare the places fairly?	Dig out soil from each place. Put it into the bowl and count the worms. How will you know that you have the same amount of soil each time?	Which bowl has most worms? What was the soil like in the place where there were most worms?
5 6 Questions and ideas	**Tests, observations & measurements**	**Evidence and explanations**
What are fair ways in which to test this idea? Is it going to be possible to collect every small animal in the area? How can you sample each area?	Make a chart to fill in whilst you are outside.	Draw different kinds of graphs to show the numbers and kinds of small animals you found in each place. What do you think would happen to the small animals if you mowed the long grass

KEY INFORMATION FOR TEACHERS

We have avoided using the term 'minibeasts', as this term has to be unlearned later (it has no particular meaning above 'small animals', and some children take it to have the same status as the word 'insect', for instance). Animals need shelter and food. All food starts with plants, and the wider variety of plants there are, the wider the variety of animals. The environment at the bottom of long grass is damp and dark, just what small animals need. Some, like woodlice, dry out and die very rapidly because they need moisture to keep their gills damp, enabling them to breathe. Many animals, like centipedes, can be found under stones where the environment is even more damp and dark.

Y1–Y2

What was the weather like yesterday? What do you think the weather will be like today?

 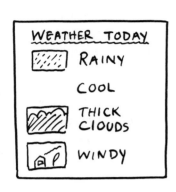 

Y3–Y4

Where do you think is the best place outside to measure the temperature? Measure the temperature each hour at three or four places. What difference do you notice?

Y5–Y6

Look at your graph showing the barometer readings for the past two weeks. What patterns can you find? Is there a connection between the rainfall and the barometer readings?

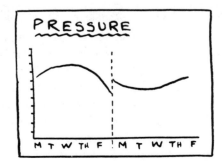 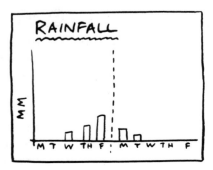

INVESTIGATING WEATHER PATTERNS

Recording the weather is best done as a short topic (about a week with young children and a month with older children). Children in years 1 and 2 can record and predict the weather in a series of drawings over a few days. Display their predictions next to pictures showing the actual weather for the same period. Children in years 3 and 4 may not have thought about the effect of direct sunshine on the temperature shown on the thermometer. The greatest temperature variations between locations will be on a sunny day. Cheap thermometers with a plastic back are best for this activity, but they are not always perfectly accurate. Try to get several which register the same temperature in the room before you begin. Barometers are instruments that you might want on permanent display in the classroom. The moveable pointer helps detect changes from one day to the next. Collect the data on atmospheric pressure over a period of two weeks as part of a topic on weather. The following boxes suggest things which teachers might say to children.

1 2 Questions and ideas	Tests, observations & measurements	Evidence and explanations
Why do you think it will stop (or start) raining? Will it stay sunny all day?	Remember to write and draw in your weather diary each day this week.	Has the weather this week been the same each day or have there been lots of changes?
3 4 Questions and ideas	Tests, observations & measurements	Evidence and explanations
Why do you think that this particular place will be colder than the other places?	Check that the thermometers all show the same temperature in the room before you start. If they don't, what will you do?	Display the results from each place side by side. What differences are there between the places? Why do you think there are these differences?
5 6 Questions and ideas	Tests, observations & measurements	Evidence and explanations
Watch the weather forecasts on the television each evening. Is there any connection between the pressure and the rainfall?	Keep a chart showing the amount of rain in the rain gauge and the air pressure each day. Make a graph of your results.	Was there any connection between changes in pressure and the amount of rainfall?

KEY INFORMATION FOR TEACHERS

Temperatures are always measured in the shade to give comparable results between different meteorological stations. Stevenson screens are built so that air can circulate within them but the thermometers are shaded from direct sunlight. Barometers measure the air pressure. The actual pressure is less important than changes from high to low pressure and vice versa. Changes to low pressure indicate the arrival of a 'low'; this often contains fronts, which are the boundaries between warm, wet air and cold, dry air. It is at these fronts that rain is most likely. There is usually a lag of about 24 hours between the arrival of the low and the main rainfall. This should be easy to see if the graphs for pressure and rainfall are set out together. If possible, use a database on a computer to record each day's weather records. You can use it to produce the graphs.

Y1–Y2

How strong is the wind today?

Y3–Y4

How can you find out which direction the wind is blowing from?

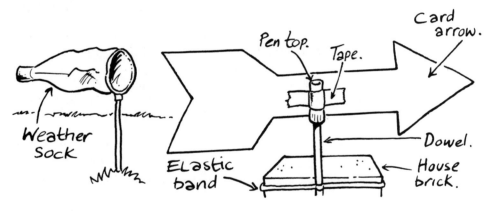

Y5–Y6

Design and make a device which will measure wind speed and another to measure wind direction. Keep records for two or three weeks. Are there any patterns in your records?

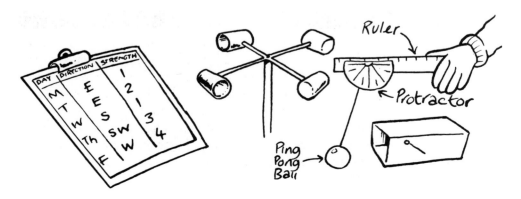

INVESTIGATING WIND

On a very windy day, let a balloon go across a big field and see the way it is carried along with the wind. Use a compass to work out the direction from which the wind is blowing. Windmills are easy to make from paper and can be held on a stick with a drawing pin. Ask year 1 and 2 children to investigate where windmills work best. Do they work best facing in a particular direction? The designs which children in years 3 and 4 might suggest include variations on wind socks, wind vanes and simple streamers. Light materials are essential for streamers or wind socks. Stiff wood or card is need for wind vanes. Find the balance point of the large indicator arrow before fixing the bearing. A wind vane or speed measurer needs a substantial base to prevent it from being blown away. A brick or large piece of wood is ideal to stop this happening. The following boxes suggest things teachers might say to children.

1 2 Questions and ideas	Tests, observations & measurements	Evidence and explanations
Which things do you think the wind can move? Which things are too heavy for it to move?	Put some plastic fizzy drinks bottles outside. Weight some down with sand or water.	Which bottles did the wind move? Which ones were too heavy for it to move? Were there places round the school where the wind didn't blow so hard?
3 4 Questions and ideas	Tests, observations & measurements	Evidence and explanations
How many different ways of measuring wind direction can you design?	Make one of your designs. Use it to work out the direction from which the wind is blowing. Compare your results with others in your class.	Which is the best type of wind direction indicator? Do you think it will be best for all strengths of wind?
5 6 Questions and ideas	Tests, observations & measurements	Evidence and explanations
Which direction do you think the wind blows from most often?	Use your wind speed and direction indicators. Record the results on a chart.	Draw graphs of the wind speed and direction.

KEY INFORMATION FOR TEACHERS

Wind is caused by the difference in air pressure between two places, which in turn is caused by the different way in which parts of the earth's surface are heated by the sun. Warm areas have rising, low-pressure air. Cooler air in the high-pressure areas falls. This descending air moves towards the low-pressure areas. The circulation round low-pressure areas is anticlockwise in the northern hemisphere and clockwise in the southern hemisphere. Wind direction is always given as the direction from which the wind is blowing. In Britain, the dominant wind direction is from the west and south-west. These winds bring rain and depressions off the Atlantic Ocean. Westerly winds have most energy and bring Britain's strongest winds. Easterly winds blow less often. In winter, they bring very cold, dry air from continental Europe. In summer, easterly winds are usually warm.

Y1–Y2

What do you think will happen when you add these kitchen powders to water?

These fizzed	Bicarbonate. Baking Powder.
These made a paste.	Washing Powder. flour.
These disappeared	Salt. Sugar.

Y3–Y4

Which of these things do you think will dissolve in water?

OUR IDEA

WE THINK THESE WILL DISSOLVE:
Salt, Sugar. flour.

WE THINK THESE WON'T DISSOLVE:
Sand, washing, Coffee.
       Powder

OUR PLAN
We will stir one spoonful into water and see what happens.

OUR TEST
We tried it and found we were wrong about flour because it settled on the bottom.

Y5–Y6

Dissolve as much Epsom salts as possible in this water. Pour it into two glasses. Put a thick piece of string in both glasses.

absorbent string

stalactite

Solution of Epsom Salts

Saucer

Our Visit to Castleton's Caverns.

INVESTIGATING POWDERS

For the year 1 and 2 activities, make sure the children are given safe powders from the kitchen. It is usually best to add the powder to the water rather than the other way round. Put dry spoons in each of the powders and keep just one spoon per group to stir with. Include some interesting powders, like baking powder, sherbet or Alka Seltzer, which will fizz when added to water. Tell them not to taste any of the powders. Children in years 3 and 4 should be asked to say how they know when something has dissolved (many of them will believe that a solid has dissolved when it has mixed in – they need to be shown that a solid is only dissolved when it has effectively disappeared in the water). Children in years 5 and 6 should already have had experience of leaving small plates of salty water to evaporate. More capable children should run several concurrent investigations of the type suggested opposite and try to make sense of them at the end of a week or so. They will find that the thick, porous string soaks up the solution more quickly than thin string. A good drying place makes the solid stalactites and stalagmites form fairly rapidly. The following boxes suggest things teachers might say to children.

	Questions and ideas	Tests, observations & measurements	Evidence and explanations
1 2	What do you think will happen to the sugar in water?	What do you think will happen when you stir it?	Which things sank to the bottom even after you stirred them?
3 4	Make a list of those things you think will dissolve and those which you think will not dissolve. How much of each powder do you think will completely dissolve in 100 ml of water?	Which material dissolves most quickly and easily? How much of each powder dissolved?	Which powders did you predict correctly? Which ones surprised you? Do you think that things which have dissolved will ever settle on the bottom again?
5 6	What do you think will happen to the water in the glasses?	What happens if you put a thinner string or perhaps a piece of plastic string in the cups? Make up two identical sets of equipment.	Explain the results of your experiments. Make sure you mention the effect of using different kinds of string.

KEY INFORMATION FOR TEACHERS

When a solid dissolves, it splits into individual molecules or atoms. These are evenly spaced throughout the solution. They will only come out of solution if the solution cools or some of the water evaporates. When solids mix with water but do not actually dissolve, the mixture is called a suspension. Flour does not dissolve but does form a suspension, and eventually the flour settles on the bottom of the container. Stalactites are formed as droplets of water containing dissolved limestone evaporate. The faster the evaporation, the faster the formation of the stalactite. Stalagmites build up from the floor by the same process.

Y1–Y2

Which of these sorts of paper do you think will mop up the spill most easily?

Y3–Y4

Design a test to see which of these papers absorbs most water.

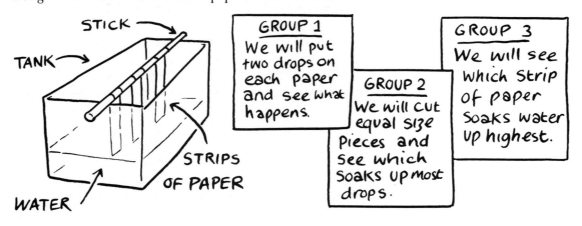

Y5–Y6

Which of these kitchen towels is the best value for money?

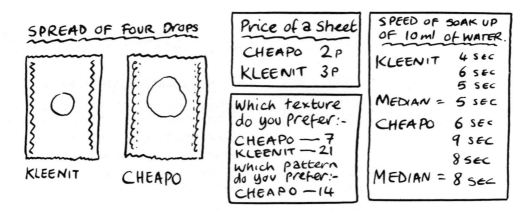

INVESTIGATING ABSORBENCY

Children in years 1 and 2 will be used to mopping up spills during art lessons. Challenge them to mop up a spill quickly, but give one child shiny magazine paper and the other absorbent newsprint or paper towel. It could become something the whole class talks about; they could go on to suggest ways in which mopping up water could be improved. There are several ways in which year 3 and 4 children could carry out their tests to find the most and least absorbent of the papers. In contrast to the younger children, they should be able to suggest plans which involve some control of the different factors. If some children place drops on the paper surface, look at the shape a drop makes. This could be extended to look at water drops on natural materials, such as feathers and leaves. The activity for children in years 5 and 6 brings another dimension into the testing of paper with the idea of value for money. Parents, shopkeepers and manufacturers may be interested in the results of the experiments. It is unlikely that all the tests, even if carried out perfectly, will show the same towel as best value. This is true to life, as the children may realise when looking at manufacturers' claims across a wide range of goods. The following boxes suggest things teachers might say to children.

1 2 Questions and ideas	Tests, observations & measurements	Evidence and explanations
Do you think this shiny paper will be any good for mopping up the spill?	Let's see which of these papers mops up the spill quickest.	Who got their part of the table dry quickest? Was it a good test?
3 4 Questions and ideas	Tests, observations & measurements	Evidence and explanations
Put the papers in order, from the one you think will be the most absorbent to the one you think will be least absorbent.	Measure the spread of each drop. How long will you wait before you do this?	On which paper does the drop spread out most?
5 6 Questions and ideas	Tests, observations & measurements	Evidence and explanations
Which of these paper towels was most expensive per sheet? What do you mean by 'best'? How could you test that? Why do you expect that one to be best? Show me your plans before you begin your tests.	How many different tests do you plan to do? Don't forget to repeat your tests if you can. How will you record your results?	Did everyone agree that this one was the best value for money?

KEY INFORMATION FOR TEACHERS

Paper absorbs water through capillary action: water is attracted to the surface of paper fibres and is drawn up into the space between them. The coarser the fibres, the more easily the paper absorbs water. Paper is made shiny by the addition of clay fillers which blocks the spaces between the fibres. Some papers, like greaseproof and baking parchment, are coated to repel water. Drops on these will form high, round buns as the water tries to get as far from the surface as possible.

Y1–Y2

Which of these bowls of water do you think will dry out most quickly?

Y3–Y4

Design a test to see which is the best place in which to dry washing.

Y5–Y6

Will a breeze from a toy fan make water evaporate more quickly than still air? Explain what you think will happen before you start your investigation.

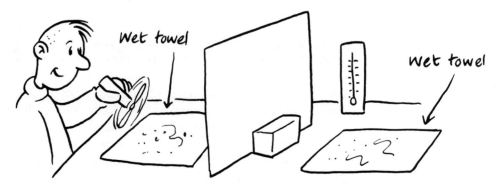

INVESTIGATING EVAPORATION

Children in years 1 and 2 may not know that evaporation happens. Some will think that water disappears because it simply soaks through the container. Investigate the effect that putting a lid on a container has on cutting down evaporation. The activity for years 3 and 4 is best done with paper towels or standard pieces of cloth. Make sure the children write on them in biro to show which towel is theirs. Gather suggestions for ways in which the amount of water on each towel can be made the same for a fair test. A dropper will be useful for this. Ensure the towels don't blow away by pegging them out or weighing them down. Some children might see the effect of folding a damp paper towel and comparing it with a spread towel. Children in years 5 and 6 can devise tests using a battery-operated fan to show how much more quickly things dry in different breezes. For instance, does it take twice as long to dry if the fan is twice as far from the cloth? The following boxes suggest things teachers might say to children.

1 2 **Questions and ideas**	**Tests, observations & measurements**	**Evidence and explanations**
What do you think will happen to the water in the bowls?	Shall we put a lid on some of these bowls? Will that be fair?	Which bowl do you think will dry out first, and which last?

3 4 **Questions and ideas**	**Tests, observations & measurements**	**Evidence and explanations**
Write a list of three places where we could dry these paper towels. Say which place you think will be best and another place where you think the towel will stay wet for a long time.	How often shall we look at the towels? When will you know that one of the towels is dry?	Why do you think this paper towel dried first? Was it the fact it was warmer here, or was it the way the wind blew?

5 6 **Questions and ideas**	**Tests, observations & measurements**	**Evidence and explanations**
Draw a diagram showing what you think happens when water evaporates. Why do you think a breeze might help to dry these water drops?	Make the drops of water on the plate the same size. What happens to the speed they dry up when you put the fan closer to them?	Design a machine which dries washing. Try to include all the things you know which will help it dry quickly.

KEY INFORMATION FOR TEACHERS

Water is the only substance which is found naturally on earth in the three states of solid, liquid and gas. It changes from a liquid to a gas through the process of evaporation. This happens most quickly when the liquid water is warm and there is a moving current of air above it. This breeze takes away the air which is saturated with water vapour and replaces it with dry air. When air is saturated with water vapour, it has a high humidity. Water does not evaporate easily in humid conditions. Water will evaporate from surfaces even when it is quite cold, as long as the humidity is low. This can be seen in fridges where food will rapidly dry out if left uncovered. Aztecs learned centuries ago that food would freeze-dry in the cold, dry air of the Andes.

Y1–Y2

What do you think is the best way to get these doll's clothes clean?

Y3–Y4

Use one sort of washing powder. Does it work best in cold water or in warm water? Does it work better if you rub the clothes for longer?

Y5–Y6

Design a test to see which of these washing powders is best at removing stains. Is there one which can clean some stains by soaking only? Are the claims made by manufacturers correct?

INVESTIGATING WASHDAY

Some children are allergic to washing powder, so have plastic gloves available. Water should be warm, not hot. The children in years 1 and 2 could apply different types of dirt to the doll's clothes (or pieces of white cotton, if you prefer). They could use school things, like crayon, glue and paint. They could also rub the cloth on the floor or grass. Let them select their own way of washing and compare the results afterwards. One of the main influences will be the vigour of the washing technique, but this could be discussed in the subsequent comparison of the results. The activity for years 3 and 4 requires the children to carry out a fair test. They should be shown the need to keep everything else the same except the temperature of the water. As a group or class, list all the things you will keep the same in the investigation. Video some soap powder advertisements for the year 5 and 6 children. Buy some of the powders mentioned and ask groups of children to carry out some of the tests the makers say they did. The results should be carefully examined, and a report written for the appropriate manufacturer. The children should work in teams investigating a particular claim made by one manufacturer. The following boxes suggest things teachers might say to children.

1 2 Questions and ideas	Tests, observations & measurements	Evidence and explanations
Do you think you can get this stain off by rubbing it in cold water?	How long will you do this for? Shall we get a sand timer?	Which stains were the most difficult to get out? Which clothes have been made cleanest?
3 4 Questions and ideas	Tests, observations & measurements	Evidence and explanations
What things should we keep the same in this test? How many temperatures shall we try? How can we make sure that no one uses water which might scald them?	Measure the temperature of this water using the thermometer. Record it on the table you have drawn.	Look at your chart. Does warmer water get the washing cleaner? Do you need to check any of the results? Were they all reliable?
5 6 Questions and ideas	Tests, observations & measurements	Evidence and explanations
What claims do the manufacturers of this powder make? How did they try to convince you that their tests were fair? Design your own test.	List the things which are going to be important in your investigation. What measuring instruments will you need?	Show your results to another group, who will act as independent experts. Do your results back up or contradict the manufacturer's claims?

KEY INFORMATION FOR TEACHERS

Many powders are detergents which lift the dirt and grease from clothes. The grease forms small balls, which are held in suspension in the water away from the clothes. Enzymes are added to biological powders. These break down proteins and loosen the dirt. They work best at specific temperatures, and soaking gives them time to act on the dirt. Some powders also contain brightening agents which reflect ultraviolet light and make the clothes look whiter. Automatic powders contain chemicals called surfactants, which cut down on the amount of lather and bubbles produced.

Y1–Y2
Draw the candle flame. What do you think will happen when your teacher puts a jar over it?

Y3–Y4
In which jar do you think the candle will burn longer?

Y5–Y6
Do you think that a candle will burn for twice as long in a jar which is twice as big as this one?

INVESTIGATING CANDLES

The candle should be held securely (use a lump of plasticine as a holder if you don't have any candle holders). Cover a sheet of stiff cardboard with kitchen foil to make a disposable, non-inflammable surface. Take the safety precautions appropriate to the age of the children. Draw the attention of year 1 and 2 children to the different colours in the candle flame. Ask them to use a range of media to draw the flame. Cover the candle with the jar on several occasions and ask the children to look out for different things each time. What do you see forming on the inside of the jar? (Condensation.) What happens just as the candle flame goes out? (A plume of white smoke goes up.) The activity for children in years 3 and 4 involves timing how long the candles burn. The children will notice that the flame goes out very quickly when you use a jar in which a candle has just been burnt. They may suggest clearing the used air from the jar by blowing into it or simply giving the used air time to disperse. Year 5 and 6 children should be able to measure the volume of each jar by filling it with water. They will need to make sure that the candle flame is the same size in each case. The following boxes suggest things teachers might say to children.

1 2	Questions and ideas	Tests, observations & measurements	Evidence and explanations
	Do you think the flame will go out straight away?	Do you think the flame will go out if we put the candle in the jar with the open end at the top?	Why do you think the candle went out?

3 4	Questions and ideas	Tests, observations & measurements	Evidence and explanations
	How can we measure the size of these jars to tell which is biggest?	How long does the candle burn in this jar. Do you think we will get exactly the same time if we do it again straight away?	Were we right about which jar would let the candle burn for longest?

5 6	Questions and ideas	Tests, observations & measurements	Evidence and explanations
	List some of the things you will need to keep the same in this experiment.	Do each measurement at least twice. What do you have to do before you use the same jar twice?	Draw a line graph to show how long the candle burns in each jar. Use it to predict how long candles will burn in this new jar.

KEY INFORMATION FOR TEACHERS

Candle wax is a hydrocarbon. That means it is composed of the chemicals hydrogen and carbon. When the candle burns, these two elements combine with oxygen to produce water and carbon dioxide. Air is a mixture of gases which includes 20% oxygen. Once the oxygen in the jar goes down to about 12%, the flame goes out. There is a direct relationship between the amount of air and the length of time a candle will burn for. The flame goes out rapidly in a jar in which a candle has just been burnt, because there is so much carbon dioxide. The same effect can be seen if you breathe out (carbon dioxide) into a jar and then place it over a candle.

Y1–Y2

What do you think will happen to this ice cube if we leave it in the warm room?

Y3–Y4

Which material wrapped around these tins keeps the water warm longest?

Y5–Y6

Do you think a full cup of tea will stay warm longer than one which is half empty? Design an investigation to find out.

INVESTIGATING TEMPERATURE CHANGE

Some children in years 1 and 2 may believe that factors other than heat are responsible for the ice melting. Some may think that light, for example, is important. (They may think that's why the freezer is so dark.) Children may not believe the standard scientific view, and you should ask them about why they think that the ice is melting. In the activity for years 3 and 4, use two sizes of tin, one inside the other. The outer one should be a great deal bigger than the other to allow for the insulating material. Cover the inner tins with card lids. Put a hole in each one large enough to take a thermometer. It is best to put one thermometer in each tin and not transfer them. Use thermometers which are mounted on a plastic back. These are usually the cheapest available and will not roll off the table. However, note that many of them only measure up to 50°C, so check that the water is cooler than that. In any case, water used in these experiments should be no hotter than 60°C to avoid scalds. With the activity for years 5 and 6, ensure that the children tell you about their plans in some detail before starting the experiment. Use a computer sensor like Measure IT, if available. The following boxes suggest things teachers might say to children.

1 2 Questions and ideas	Tests, observations & measurements	Evidence and explanations
Why do you think ice cubes melt when they are out of the freezer?	Let's wrap this ice cube in a towel. Will it make any difference if we stand one ice cube on a plate above a radiator?	Look at the ice cubes after half an hour. Which has melted most? Which is largest?
3 4 Questions and ideas	Tests, observations & measurements	Evidence and explanations
Which of these materials do you think will be the best at keeping the can warm?	Keep a careful note of the temperature in each container every two minutes.	Draw a graph showing the way the temperature changed. Which wrapping kept the water warm longest?
5 6 Questions and ideas	Tests, observations & measurements	Evidence and explanations
Which temperature should we start the water at? How long shall we do the measurements for? Would it be better to wait until one of the cups has cooled to a particular temperature?	Which container will you use? Is it important to use the same sort and size of container each time?	Draw a graph showing the results you got. Predict how long it will take 200 ml of water which starts at 60°C to reach 30°C.

KEY INFORMATION FOR TEACHERS

Warm water will cool down and ice cubes will heat up until they are the same temperature as the surrounding air and objects. Materials like metals are very good conductors of heat, whereas sponge or fluffy fabrics do not pass on heat very well at all.

Much heat is lost when steam evaporates off the surface of warm water. A lid slows this process down. A large amount of water holds its heat well because it has a small surface area from which to lose heat.

Y1–Y2

Which of these two balls is the best bouncer?

Y3–Y4

Which of these balls bounces highest on this sort of floor?

Y5–Y6

Predict which ball will bounce highest on this floor. Do you think the same ball will bounce highest on all sorts of surface?

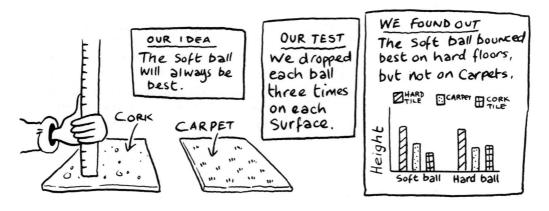

INVESTIGATING BOUNCING BALLS

In all these activities, use different types of balls (which might include tennis balls, sponge balls and rubber balls). Discuss with children whether they will do their measurements at the top or the bottom of the ball. The year 1 and 2 activity can be included as part of a PE session. The children can pat the balls, drop them or try to make them bounce as high as possible. Children in years 3 and 4 should be encouraged to plan fair tests where they can change one thing systematically. In this case, the floor should be the same for all the investigations carried out by one group. They should be shown how to repeat their measurements to get consistent results. Show the children how to take a median (this is the middle value of a set of results and is much easier to calculate than an average). If a ball bounces 50 cm, 45 cm and 56 cm, then 50 cm is the median reading. In the activity for years 5 and 6, be prepared for some inconsistent results. The ball which bounced highest on a hard surface will not necessarily bounce highest on a soft surface. The following boxes suggest things teachers might say to children.

1 2 Questions and ideas	Tests, observations & measurements	Evidence and explanations
Do you think this very squashy ball will bounce well?	How high can you make this ball bounce? Does it go as high as the other one?	Which ball is the best for playing bounce and catch between two people?
3 4 Questions and ideas	Tests, observations & measurements	Evidence and explanations
Do you think it will be important to make sure that all balls are dropped in the same way?	Do each measurement three times. Will you measure the top of the ball or the bottom of the ball?	Look at other people's results. Does everyone think the same ball is the best bouncer?
5 6 Questions and ideas	Tests, observations & measurements	Evidence and explanations
Do you think you will get the same results on each type of floor surface? Will this ball always be the bounciest?	Will you measure the height of the first bounce, or the number of bounces the ball makes?	Are the results clear? Does the same ball bounce best on each type of surface? Is one ball always the worst bouncer?

KEY INFORMATION FOR TEACHERS

Balls bounce because they are elastic. When a ball is lifted up to about shoulder height, it is given potential energy. When it is dropped, the ball's potential energy is changed into kinetic energy (movement energy). The force with which the ball hits the ground changes its shape. This gives the ball a different form of stored energy (elastic strain energy). Because the ball is elastic, it rapidly recovers its original shape and is pushed back upwards. If the floor onto which the ball falls is very soft and squashy, it will absorb the energy of the fall, and the ball may bounce back very little. The interplay between the ball's elasticity and the way the floor absorbs the energy makes it very difficult to predict the outcome of the activity. The children may be surprised when hard balls bounce well on very hard tiled surfaces. All materials are elastic to some degree.

Y1–Y2

Use a balloon to make this toy fall more slowly.

Y3–Y4

Investigate which is the best material to make a parachute from.

Y5–Y6

Find out which factors are important in the way parachutes fall.

INVESTIGATING PARACHUTES

Children in years 1 and 2 will find making parachutes difficult, so any light object with a large surface area can be used to slow the fall of the toy. Large balloons with a big surface area will slow the toy's fall dramatically. The best material for making parachute canopies is thin plastic from carrier bags or bin liners. Tissue paper is good, but it tends to be fragile. Use very thin string or strong cotton thread to make the ties. It is difficult to time the fall of the parachutes unless you have access to a long, safe drop. In years 3 and 4, the children should be asked to investigate one variable, with the others largely controlled through the teacher's instruction. A class of co-operative year 5 and 6 pupils could list some of the variables which affect the parachute's fall and divide the task of investigating different variables between themselves. In this investigation, the independent variables include: weight of load, weight of parachute, area of parachute, shape of parachute, the degree to which the canopy opens fully and whether air can get through the material of the canopy. The following boxes suggest things teachers might say to children.

1 2 Questions and ideas	Tests, observations & measurements	Evidence and explanations
Do you think a balloon which wasn't blown up would make the toy fall slowly?	What do you think would happen if we dropped a heavier object with this balloon?	Which balloon gave the toy the softest landing?
3 4 Questions and ideas	Tests, observations & measurements	Evidence and explanations
Do you think this net curtain material will make a good parachute? What about this light, plastic material? Why do you think this?	Which things are you going to keep the same in this investigation? How will you tell which parachute works best?	Make a display showing which material made the best parachute. Did all your friends get a similar result? If not, what do you think could be the reason for that?
5 6 Questions and ideas	Tests, observations & measurements	Evidence and explanations
Do you think square, circular or rectangular parachutes will work best? Some people say that a small hole at the top of the parachute helps it fall more slowly. Is this correct?	Which of these parachutes has the biggest surface area? Does that make any difference?	Describe the ideal toy parachute. What should it be made from, what shape should it be and should there be a hole at the top?

KEY INFORMATION FOR TEACHERS

Light objects with large surface areas, such as balloons or parachutes, are slowed by air resistance. The lighter the object and the bigger its surface area, the slower it falls. This is why parachutes made from light material such as tissue fall so slowly. A hole up to the size of a 5p coin allows air to escape from a parachute's canopy in a controlled way. The air inside the parachute is at a higher pressure than the air outside.

Y1–Y2
Watch how these very light objects fall.

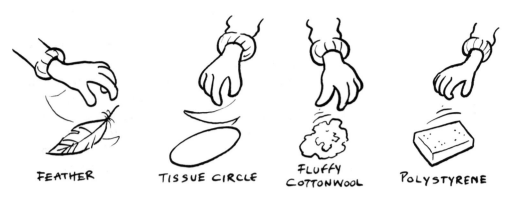

FEATHER   TISSUE CIRCLE   FLUFFY COTTONWOOL   POLYSTYRENE

Y3–Y4
What can you do to make this piece of paper fall slowly? What can you do to speed it up?

I think the crumpled piece will fall faster.

Paper on its edge will slide through the air.

I think making lots of cuts on one piece will slow it down

Y5–Y6
Collect some very light objects. Which will fall slowest? Put them in order from those which you think will fall fastest to those which you think will fall most slowly. Do a careful test to see if you were right.

WE THINK THE TISSUE WILL FALL SLOWEST BECAUSE OF AIR RESISTANCE.

WE ARE GOING TO TEST IF SMALL PIECES FALL FASTER THAN LARGE PIECES.

We are going to tear holes in paper. Some people think the holes will make the paper drop faster.

Quickest — our Predictions — Slowest

tile   String   cotton wool   tissue

INVESTIGATING LIGHT OBJECTS

In the activity for years 1 and 2, use things like tissue circles and very light, downy feathers. The circles twirl around in unpredictable ways, whereas the feather or fluffed-out pieces of cotton wool fall straight down (unless blown by draughts). If working outdoors, look at the way in which different leaves and tree seeds fall. In the year 3 and 4 activity, the paper can be folded or crumpled in order to make it fall more quickly. This changes its surface area and reduces the air resistance, which slows the fall of the paper. If the paper is dropped flat, this maximises its air resistance, so it drops slowly. When dropped edge on, its air resistance is greatly reduced. Do these dropping experiments over a relatively short drop of about one metre. If you do it from higher up, the drop is far less reliable. The year 5 and 6 activities require very light objects like feathers, strands of cotton, pieces of tissue and fluffy pieces of kapok or cotton wool. The following boxes suggest things teachers might say to children.

1 2 Questions and ideas	Tests, observations & measurements	Evidence and explanations
Which of these things do you think will twirl round as it falls? Which do you think will fall straight down?	Cut the tissue circle in half. How does that affect the way in which it falls?	Draw pictures showing the way some of the things fell.
3 4 Questions and ideas	Tests, observations & measurements	Evidence and explanations
Do you think the paper will fall more slowly if you cut the edges into a fringe?	Watch carefully to see if dropping the paper flat or edge first makes a difference.	Make a list of the things you did and the effect they had. Was it easier to slow the fall of the paper or to speed it up?
5 6 Questions and ideas	Tests, observations & measurements	Evidence and explanations
What force do you think slows the fall of the very light objects, like the feather? In which direction must it be acting?	Does it matter if you drop all the objects from different heights? Can you design a test so that you don't have to try and drop all the objects at the same time?	Why do you think these objects fall so slowly? Find out about terminal velocity. Which things have very high terminal velocities?

KEY INFORMATION FOR TEACHERS

Air resistance slows the fall of objects. If there was no air, all objects, no matter what their size or weight, would fall at the same rate. On the moon, where there is gravity but no air, a feather and a hammer fall at the same speed and will land at the same time. The main factor affecting the fall of pieces of paper is air resistance. Lowering the air resistance by folding the paper or screwing it into a ball causes the paper to fall faster. Very light objects, such as feathers and fluff, do not continue to speed up during their fall. This is because, once they begin to fall, the air resistance is equal to the pull of gravity. In other words, they have reached their terminal velocity.

Y1–Y2

Play with this paper gyrocopter. What seed does it remind you of?

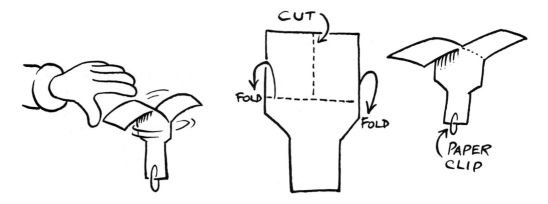

Y3–Y4

Does it make any difference to the way the gyrocopter falls if you make the wings shorter? What happens when you add more paper clips to the bottom?

Y5–Y6

Plan an investigation into the things which make a really good gyrocopter. For instance, what is the ideal number of clips or the best paper to make it with? Share out the experiments and bring all your results together.

INVESTIGATING GYROCOPTERS

Gyrocopters are easy to make, and the variables are simple to manipulate. The year 1 and 2 activity suggests that the children start by playing with their gyrocopters – this is a good way to start with any group. If it is autumn, bring in sycamore and ash seeds, which fall in a similar way to gyrocopters. The activity for years 3 and 4 would be even more productive if the children came up with their own suggestions for altering the gyrocopter rather than simply responding to their teacher's ideas. The children should alter only one thing at a time so they can make sense

of their results at the end of the work. The activity for years 5 and 6 relies on the children working in separate teams, which combine results and ideas at the end of their initial work. They should find that no weight on the bottom causes the gyrocopter to fall without spinning, yet too much makes it fall more rapidly. The type of paper used is important; tissue may be light, but it is too floppy to be the ideal gyrocopter paper. The following boxes suggest things teachers might say to children.

1 2 Questions and ideas	Tests, observations & measurements	Evidence and explanations
Do you think you could make it spin in the other direction?	Try changing over the way the wings are folded. Put a big red dot on one of them to help you see which way it is turning.	Draw a picture showing the way the gyrocopter twisted. Write a sentence saying what you did and what happened.
3 4 Questions and ideas	Tests, observations & measurements	Evidence and explanations
What ideas do you have about the things that will affect the way the gyrocopter falls?	Make two gyrocopters and load one with two paper clips and the other with one paper clip. Can you make them land together when dropped from the same height at the same time?	Make a table showing each thing you did and the effect it had on the way the gyrocopter fell.
5 6 Questions and ideas	Tests, observations & measurements	Evidence and explanations
What is your group going to investigate? Write it down, so we can discuss it. Do you have any ideas about what would make the best gyrocopter?	Make sure you keep everything else the same when you are changing something (for example, the paper that the gyrocopter is made from).	Each group should go away now and use all the results to design the best gyrocopter. Do you think all our designs will be identical?

KEY INFORMATION FOR TEACHERS

The reason why the gyrocopter spins in one direction rather than another is difficult to explain. Clearly the fold of the wings causes it to spin in a particular direction, but that is only a partial explanation. Saying that you don't know is probably the most honest response for most people. That shouldn't diminish your standing with pupils, as most of them

respect honesty! It also makes the point that you can investigate productively even when the basic science is not completely understood. The area of the wings is one of the most important factors governing the fall of the gyrocopter, with large areas offering greatest air resistance and therefore slowest rates of fall.

Y1–Y2

Use these objects to see which float and which sink.

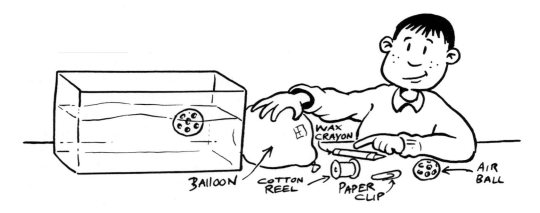

Y3–Y4

Use these objects. Predict which you think will float. Give your reasons.

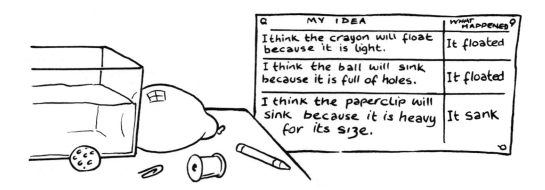

Q	MY IDEA	WHAT HAPPENED?
	I think the crayon will float because it is light.	It floated
	I think the ball will sink because it is full of holes.	It floated
	I think the paperclip will sink because it is heavy for its size.	It sank

Y5–Y6

Look at this diver in the bottle. Investigate why it sinks and floats. Can you make it hover in the middle of the bottle?

INVESTIGATING WHY THINGS FLOAT

The activity for years 1 and 2 asks children to observe objects in water. This is best done through a clear plastic aquarium. At this stage, most children will say that light things float and heavy things sink. Give them some small dense objects and some objects which are light for their size to challenge this idea. Encourage observational drawing in this activity. By years 3 and 4, most children should be able to suggest a number of reasons why some things float and others sink. Good hypotheses include: 'It's got air in it', 'It's light for its size', 'The water pushes back'. Ask them to think of ways to test their ideas. They might, for instance, want to see if all objects which contain air float. Children in years 5 and 6 find the diver made from a dropper pipette fascinating. Either a plastic or a glass and rubber dropper pipette will do. When preparing the activity, make sure that you try the dropper in a wide jug first. Make the dropper heavier by drawing in water and adding paper clips to the tube. When it just floats in the jug put it in the plastic bottle. Put the lid on the plastic bottle and squeeze the sides of the bottle and the dropper will sink. Let go of the sides and the dropper will rise to the surface. The following boxes suggest questions teachers might ask at each stage.

1 2	Questions and ideas	Tests, observations & measurements	Evidence and explanations
	Which do you think will sink? Which do you think will float?	Draw a picture showing which things float and which sink.	Use your picture to tell me which sunk.
3 4	Questions and ideas	Tests, observations & measurements	Evidence and explanations
	Why do you think that one will sink?	Test each one in turn. Make a table showing what happened.	Were you right? Which things were you wrong about? Do you still have the same idea about why things float or sink?
5 6	Questions and ideas	Tests, observations & measurements	Evidence and explanations
	What do you think you have to do to make the diver sink? What possible explanations could there be for it sinking?	Do investigations testing each of your ideas in turn. Make notes about what you notice.	Does your explanation convince the rest of the group?

KEY INFORMATION FOR TEACHERS

Objects which are light for their size, for example rubber balls and corks, will float. Objects which are heavy for their size, for example rubber bands and paper clips, will sink. Heavy candles float and are likely to challenge the idea that only light objects and those which contain air will float. Things sink if they are denser than water. The diver sinks when you squeeze the bottle because the air in the pipette is squashed and its place is taken by water which is much heavier than the air. When the diver hovers in the middle of the bottle it has the same weight as an identical volume of water. In other words, the whole diver has the same density as water.

Y1–Y2

How could a clever bird get a drink from this half-full bottle?

Y3–Y4

Who has got the biggest hand in the class? How many ways can you think of to measure hands?

Y5–Y6

How much water does this object push out of the way when it is floating? What happens when you push it under the water?

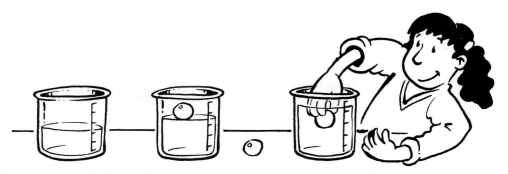

INVESTIGATING DISPLACEMENT

The activity for years 1 and 2 is taken from Aesop's fable about the thirsty crow which dropped stones into a narrow pitcher to make the water rise. Give the children simple investigations, such as finding out how many pebbles they need to overflow water from a half-full jug. Ask them what they expect to happen when you put an object into a nearly full container. Use a plastic bottle in case a child suggests using a pebble to smash the bottle! If you fill a 1000 ml (1 litre) measuring container to an easy number, for example 500 ml, then year 3 and 4 children should have relatively little problem in working out the volume of water displaced by objects. Alternatively, they could simply record the level to which the water rose in each case. They can use this method to find the volume of other irregular objects, such as hands. Challenge them to make the test fair by agreeing on a standard place where the water should come up to on each person's wrist. The year 5 and 6 example needs clear, calibrated measuring jugs of varying size. The children should be encouraged to choose the right size jug to measure the displacement of different size objects, for example rubber balls. You may need a sensitive electronic scale to find their mass. These are surprisingly cheap. The following boxes suggest questions teachers might ask at each stage.

1 2 Questions and ideas	Tests, observations & measurements	Evidence and explanations
If the bird got some small stones, how could it use them to get at the water?	Try out some of your ideas.	Why do the stones make the water rise in the bottle? What happens to the water level when you get into the bath?
3 4 Questions and ideas	Tests, observations & measurements	Evidence and explanations
Will big hands make the water level rise more than small hands?	Make a table of your results. How did you make sure the test was fair for everyone?	How could you measure the volume of different pieces of rock?
5 6 Questions and ideas	Tests, observations & measurements	Evidence and explanations
Do you think there is any connection between the weight of this object and the amount of water it displaces when it floats?	Record your results on a table. Do it for at least three floating objects.	Write out a rule which explains what you notice. Do you think the results are more accurate if you use a container which is just a bit bigger than the object?

KEY INFORMATION FOR TEACHERS

Displacement is a critical idea in understanding why things float. When an object goes into water it displaces water. The greater volume an object has below the surface of the water the more water it displaces. A floating object displaces some water. When you push it under the water, more is displaced.

Able children will notice that a floating ball which has a mass of 70 g will displace 70 ml of water. This volume of water has a mass of 70 g. Very able children may move towards an understanding that a floating object displaces its own weight of water.

Y1–Y2
Feel the water push back when you try to push this balloon under the water.

Y3–Y4
How far does this stone stretch the elastic band? How far does it stretch when you gently lower the stone into the water? Don't rest it on the bottom.

Y5–Y6
Weigh these objects using a spring balance. What do you think will happen to their weight when they are under water? Don't rest them on the bottom.

OBJECT	WEIGHT IN AIR	WEIGHT IN WATER	VOLUME DISPLACED
STONE	250 g	150 g	100 ml
BRICK	200 g	120 g	80 ml
WOOD	220 g	0 g	220 ml

INVESTIGATING UPTHRUST

The activity for years 1 and 2 is probably best done as a whole class with all the children taking turns to feel the push back (upthrust) from the water. Get them to notice how the push back increases as more water is displaced. If you let the children work in small groups, you risk a minor flood, unless it can be done outdoors. In the year 3 and 4 activity, try to avoid using porous bricks or rocks which bubble in water. This phenomenon is interesting, but would lead you into other scientific investigations which you might prefer to leave for another day. The

difference in the stretch on the rubber band is most noticeable as you lift the rock out of the water. Don't use metal masses, as these do not show such a dramatic effect. If you take the children swimming, get them to feel heavy life saving bricks in and out of the water. For the year 5 and 6 activity use spring balances calibrated in newtons if you have them. However, spring balances calibrated in grams are acceptable. Make sure that the children don't rest the stone on the bottom of the tank. The following boxes suggest things teachers might say to children.

1 2 Questions and ideas	Tests, observations & measurements	Evidence and explanations
Do you think it will be easy to push the balloon under the water?	Find out if it is easier to push a smaller balloon into the water.	Why do you think the water pushes the big balloon so much?
3 4 Questions and ideas	Tests, observations & measurements	Evidence and explanations
What do you think will happen to the stretch on the elastic band when you put different objects into the water?	Which objects make the elastic band go completely slack?	Why do you think the elastic band stretches less when an object is in water?
5 6 Questions and ideas	Tests, observations & measurements	Evidence and explanations
Predict what will happen to the weight of the objects when they are in the water.	Make a table to record your results.	What sort of objects lose all their weight? Which ones lose least weight?

KEY INFORMATION FOR TEACHERS

The amount of force needed to push the balloon under water increases with the amount of water displaced. The children should be able to feel that the water pushes back as the balloon displaces more water. A smaller balloon or ball will produce less push back (upthrust) because it displaces less water. The stretch on the elastic band is less when the object is in the

water because the object displaces water and gets some upthrust from the water. Objects which float appear to lose weight in water. This weight loss is equal to the weight of water the object displaces. Things which float lose all their weight and register no weight on a spring balance.

Y1–Y2

Use these containers as boats. Load them with marbles.

Y3–Y4

Make boat shapes from foil. Which shape carries most weight?

Y5–Y6

Make two or three plasticine boats. Weigh them. How much water does each displace?

INVESTIGATING BOATS

Polystyrene food trays, margarine tubs and the lids from plastic containers make good boats. Activities like this are great fun, and, in years 1 and 2, it is sensible to allow directed play before embarking on the more focused scientific investigations. Children should notice that, when a load is put into the boat, it sinks lower in the water. Give the children in years 3 and 4 equal-size pieces of foil and get them to make boats with tall sides and shallow sides. The plasticine used in the year 5 and 6 activity can present problems because of the thickness of the boat's sides, but by this time, children should be able to see how to make them. A calibrated measuring container which is only a little larger than the boat will give the most accurate reading of the water displaced. The following boxes suggest things teachers might say to children.

	Questions and ideas	Tests, observations & measurements	Evidence and explanations
1 2	Which container do you think will carry most marbles? Why do you think that?	What happens if you cut a piece out of the rim of the container?	Why did that container carry most weight? Why did that one carry least marbles?
3 4	Which shape do you predict will carry most weight? Write your predictions in the table.	How will you make sure the test is fair? Make them all from the same size piece of foil. Use your table to record the shapes and weights.	Is there any connection between the volume of water the boats hold and the weight of the cargo they can carry?
5 6	Do you think there will be any connection between the weight of a boat and the amount of water it displaces?	Try your investigation. What is the best equipment to use? Record your results.	Is the equipment accurate enough for this investigation? Is there another way to do it?

KEY INFORMATION FOR TEACHERS

As a load is placed on a boat, it sinks lower in the water. When a boat sinks lower in the water, the volume of water it displaces is increased. There is always a balance between the weight of the water displaced and the weight of the boat. Forces can be shown by drawing arrows. A downwards-pointing arrow represents the weight of the object. An arrow drawn to show the force upwards on a floating object will be the same length as the arrow representing its weight. Plasticine or foil boats with a greater volume hold more cargo because they are capable of displacing more water. However, be careful to distinguish between the boat's internal capacity and the volume which it will displace. This takes account of the thickness of the sides. Many children wrongly believe that surface area is an important factor in floating. The factor to focus on is the volume of water displaced. The weight of a ship is often referred to as its displacement.

Y1–Y2

Make a bulb light using a bulb, a piece of wire or foil and a single cell. Now put the bulb and cell in holders, use two pieces of wire. Make the bulb light.

Y3–Y4

Make a series circuit where several bulbs are connected together.

Y5–Y6

Make series circuits which use different numbers of bulbs and cells. How bright are the bulbs in each circuit you make?

BATTERY VOLTAGE	VOLTAGE OF BULB	BRIGHTNESS
1·5 v	2·5 v	2
1·5 v	3·5 v	2
1·5 v	6 v	1
3 v	6 v	

INVESTIGATING BATTERIES AND BULBS

The year 1 and 2 activity uses the simplest possible equipment, so that children are not daunted initially by the need for special holders. The first part draws attention to the two connections on the bulb, which are the brass screw and the silver pip at the base of the bulb. Most children will work hard at the activity for some time, trying a variety of ways to get the bulb to light. There are no safety worries, provided they do not use rechargeable cells. When making series circuits with children in years 3 and 4, ensure that the bulbs come from the same packet, or you may find there are odd results to explain, with some bulbs glowing more brightly than others. The year 5 and 6 investigation involves the manipulation of several variables, namely the voltage of the cells and different combinations of bulbs. The children should try to distinguish between them by keeping the battery voltage the same whilst altering the voltage of the bulb or combination of the bulbs. The following boxes suggest things teachers might say to children.

1 2 **Questions and ideas**	**Tests, observations & measurements**	**Evidence and explanations**
How do you think you could light the bulb?	Are there any other ways you could make the bulb light?	Do you always need a wire from both ends of the cell?
3 4 **Questions and ideas**	**Tests, observations & measurements**	**Evidence and explanations**
Do you think the number of bulbs you connect up to this cell will make any difference to their brightness?	What will happen in this circuit when you unscrew one of the bulbs?	Why do you think the other bulb in the circuit went out when you unscrewed the first one?
5 6 **Questions and ideas**	**Tests, observations & measurements**	**Evidence and explanations**
Investigate the effect of using two or three cells in series with one bulb. Investigate the effect of using a bulb of different voltage.	Make a table to record what happened in your investigation. Try swapping over the position in the circuit of the (different voltage) bulbs. What do you think might happen to the bulb if you used four cells in series?	Why do you think two cells in series make the bulb glow so brightly? Why do you think that the 6 v bulb was dimmer than the 2.5 v bulb? Does the brightness of the bulbs depend on their position or on the bulb itself?

KEY INFORMATION FOR TEACHERS

Cells are the barrel-shaped things often called batteries. A battery is a group of cells wired together. Bulbs glow because the very thin filament in the bulb resists the flow of electricity through it. A high-voltage bulb will only glow brightly if connected to a high-voltage battery. Low-voltage bulbs will break if connected to a high-voltage battery: the filament melts. Add the voltage of two batteries placed in series (one after the other). Unscrewing one bulb in a series circuit leads to the other one going out, as electricity no longer flows. In a series circuit, the position of the bulb is not important. A bulb which glows brightly in one position in the circuit will also glow brightly in another position.

Y1–Y2

Make simple circuits to test things to see if electricity will pass through.

Y3–Y4

Make a simple circuit. Investigate the effect that a pencil lead has on the flow of electricity.

Y5–Y6

Investigate the way in which resistance wire works. What do you think will happen to the brightness of the bulb if you use two strands of resistance wire side by side?

INVESTIGATING CONDUCTORS AND INSULATORS

Remind children that small batteries are safe but mains electricity can be fatal.

When year 1 and 2 children are exploring whether an object conducts electricity, they will notice that most metal objects conduct. However, remember that painted or dirty metal may not conduct. Objects such as wire coat hangers are coated with lacquer which prevents the electricity flowing. This inconvenience could be turned into an investigation by asking the children to try to find out why some metal objects do not conduct electricity. When preparing the pencil lead for

the year 3 and 4 activity, use a sharp knife and take great care to cut away from fingers or use propelling pencil leads. Use crocodile clips to grip the pencil lead. You are unlikely to make a good enough contact by simply rubbing a wire on the lead. Resistance wire resists the electricity. You can get this wire from many educational suppliers under the name nichrome wire or constantan. Alternatively, prior to the lesson, get some heating element wire from an old heater. The following boxes suggest things teachers might say to children.

1 2 Questions and ideas	Tests, observations & measurements	Evidence and explanations
Do you think the bulb will light if you put this paper clip in the circuit? What other things will the bulb light with?	Try them and find out. Fill in the table to record what you notice.	Let's look at your table. Tell me which objects let the electricity through. Is there anything special about these objects?
3 4 Questions and ideas	Tests, observations & measurements	Evidence and explanations
What do you think will happen to the bulb when you connect the pencil lead into the circuit?	Try connecting it up so the electricity has to run through different lengths of lead.	Why do you think the bulb went dimmer? What do you think pencil lead does to the flow of electricity?
5 6 Questions and ideas	Tests, observations & measurements	Evidence and explanations
What effect do you think that resistance wire will have in the circuit?	Record the changes you notice when you double the length of the wire and then when you use two wire strands side by side.	Do you think using three or four strands would make that effect even more obvious? Why does it work like this?

KEY INFORMATION FOR TEACHERS

Conductors conduct electricity because they have free electrons which carry the charge. Insulators, like plastic and wood, do not have free electrons. Graphite (pencil lead) and resistance wire allow some electricity to flow. Constantan wire is made of a metal which restricts the flow of electricity. This type of wire has many uses, including heating elements in

electrical heaters. Fuse wire is a type of resistance wire. It gets hot when electricity passes through it and can melt if there is excess current. The greater the length of resistance wire, the less electricity flows. Putting two pieces of resistance wire side by side halves the resistance because there is double the thickness of wire for the electricity to pass through.

Y1–Y2
Which things are attracted to this magnet?

Y3–Y4
Which magnet is strongest?

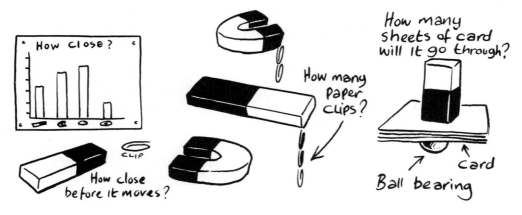

Y5–Y6
Design a test to find out which part of the magnet is strongest.

INVESTIGATING MAGNETIC STRENGTH

Buying strong magnets in the first place is important. Ceramic magnets maintain their strength without the use of keepers. They are also cased in bright plastic. Magnetism is an ideal topic for interactive display, where the children can use the equipment when they have spare moments. Look at devices which use magnets. These include fridge door seals and magnetic letters. There are several approaches to testing the strength of individual magnets or parts of magnets that year 3 and 4 children might adopt.

Get them to follow up their own approaches. Measuring the force (usually in the form of weight) needed to pull an object away from a magnet is one way. Measuring the distance over which a magnet attracts an object is another. By years 5 and 6, the children should be able to suggest several ways of doing their test before they actually handle the equipment. This could be done in the form of simple sketches rather than laboured pieces of writing. The following boxes suggest things teachers might say to children.

1 2	Questions and ideas	Tests, observations & measurements	Evidence and explanations
	What sort of things do you think will be attracted to the magnet?	Are the paper clips attracted to the magnet through paper?	Are all metals attracted to magnets?
3 4	**Questions and ideas**	**Tests, observations & measurements**	**Evidence and explanations**
	Do you expect the biggest magnet to be the strongest?	Write a list of as many ways you can think of to test the strength of the magnets. Try one or two of your tests.	Does one magnet always seem to be the strongest in all your tests? Which magnet is the best one to buy for use in school?
5 6	**Questions and ideas**	**Tests, observations & measurements**	**Evidence and explanations**
	Where would you expect most small nails to stick to the magnet? Why do you think that?	Is this the same for all sorts of magnets, including horseshoe and circular ones?	Find a diagram in a book which shows the lines of force made by a magnet. Where are they most concentrated, at the poles or at the middle?

KEY INFORMATION FOR TEACHERS

Both iron and steel are attracted to magnets. No other metals commonly found in schools are magnetic. Magnetic force can pass through most materials. A strong magnet will easily attract objects though a thick plank of wood. Iron will shield magnetism, but if either the magnet or the object is touching the iron, the shielding no longer works. The piece of iron itself becomes a magnet (induced magnetism) if the magnet

is touching it. Magnetic lines of force are concentrated at the poles. This is easily demonstrated when iron filings in a sealed container concentrate at the poles. Note, too, how the filings stand up at the poles yet lie down at the equator of the magnet. The density of magnetic force varies greatly from magnet to magnet and the largest is not necessarily the strongest.

Y1–Y2

What happens when you bring one end of the magnet toward another magnet? Look at these circular magnets on a stick. Why do you think they are not touching? Do you think you could make them touch?

Y3–Y4

In which direction do you expect this bar magnet will point when you rest it on a floating plate?

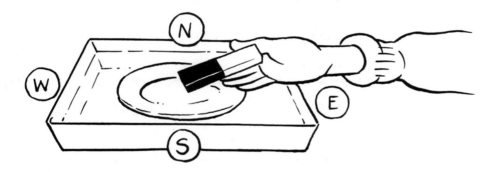

Y5–Y6

Stroke this pin twenty times with the north pole of this magnet. Fix it on the card. In which direction do you think it will point?

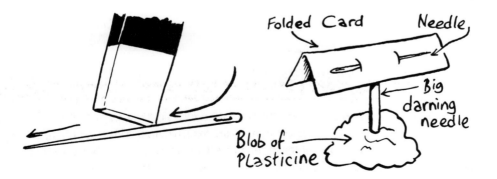

INVESTIGATING COMPASSES

The polo magnets (circular with a hole in the middle) used in the year 1 and 2 activity give an excellent sensation of the repulsion between two like poles. The closer the children push them together, the harder they push apart. They are relatively fragile and may break if dropped. Store them in stacks so they stick together. Unlike bar magnets, the poles of the polo magnets and some of the small magnets are on the flat faces rather than the ends. In the year 3 and 4 investigation, make sure that the floating bar magnet is well away from the iron table frame and any other magnets. Bring another magnet about 50 cm away from the floating magnet. Notice that the same pole repels and the opposite pole attracts. There are only a few variables involved in exploring magnetism, but they do demand clear logic. Most magnets are coloured red at the north pole and blue at the south pole. The following boxes suggest things teachers might say to children.

1 2 Questions and ideas	Tests, observations & measurements	Evidence and explanations
What do you think will happen when you push the polo-shaped magnets together?	Try turning the magnets round. What do you notice?	Draw a picture of two magnets which attract each other. Draw a picture of two magnets which push each other apart.
3 4 Questions and ideas	Tests, observations & measurements	Evidence and explanations
How do you think magnetic compasses work?	Use a bought compass to check the direction in which your floating magnet is pointing. Do compasses always point in the right direction if there are magnets nearby?	If you took your floating magnet outside, do you think it would still point in the same direction?
5 6 Questions and ideas	Tests, observations & measurements	Evidence and explanations
Now you have seen the direction the pin points when you stroked it with the north pole, what do you think will happen if you stroke it in the same way with the south pole?	What other ways could you stroke the pin? Find out what happens if you stroke it in the opposite direction.	Do you think it would be possible to make a compass from a pin and a horseshoe magnet. If not, why not?

KEY INFORMATION FOR TEACHERS

The earth's magnetic field behaves as if it had a bar magnet running through the centre. The south pole of this magnet is at the north geographical pole. The north pole of the magnet floating in a dish will seek the earth's geographical north pole. The direction of a pin's magnetism is affected by the pole which does the stroking and the direction in which it is stroked. The activities at Key Stage 2 involve turning a piece of steel into a magnet by stroking. This is called 'induced magnetism'. Steel needles hold magnetism well, but iron nails do not remain magnetic once out of physical contact with a magnet.

Y1–Y2

Feel things in the bag. What can you say about them? Take one out of the bag. Look carefully at it. What else can you say about it now?

Y3–Y4

Find out how accurate you are at throwing a beanbag into a bucket. See how your score changes when you shut one eye.

Y5–Y6

Have you ever had your eyes tested with a chart like this? Make up your own charts to test eyesight. Find out which works best.

INVESTIGATING SIGHT

If there are pupils who are partially sighted, similar skills can be developed through the investigation of other senses, such as touch and hearing. Pupils in years 1 and 2 can compare the different sorts of information we get from our various senses and realise how much we depend on sight. Ask them to justify their predictions and check the evidence when they describe or identify objects in a feely bag. Children in years 3 and 4 could develop their own tests to investigate how much their judgement of distance is better with two eyes than one, for example when throwing a beanbag into a bucket. They should repeat tests to check their results, record them systematically (for example, on a prepared table) and evaluate the tests they did by talking about possible improvements (for example, testing at different distances). By years 5 and 6, children should be able to design their own tests and carry out a whole investigation to compare eyecharts, for example using figures or pictures. They will need to consider what to measure, how many pupils to test, how to record their measurements during the investigation and how to present and summarise their results. This might be in a table displayed with the charts they tested. The following boxes suggest things teachers might say to children.

1 2	Questions and ideas	Tests, observations & measurements	Evidence and explanations
	What can you feel? What do you think it is? Tell us what you think it will look like.	Were you right? What more can you tell us about it now you can see it? Feel something else. What can you say about it just by feeling?	What do your eyes tell you that you cannot find out just by feeling? What can't you find out just by looking at something?
3 4	Questions and ideas	Tests, observations & measurements	Evidence and explanations
	What do you need two eyes for? What difference does it make if you close one? Will you be able to throw as accurately?	What was your score? Test someone else. How far away was the bucket? What else could you use instead of the bucket and beanbag?	How much difference did it make using two eyes instead of one? Why do you think it makes a difference? Would your results be the same if you changed the distance?
5 6	Questions and ideas	Tests, observations & measurements	Evidence and explanations
	What else could you put on a sight chart instead of letters? Do you think it will make any difference? Why do you think so?	What will you measure each time? How far away should the chart be when you start? How will you check that they really can see what they say?	Which test worked best? Did you get the same results with each eye? Were the results the same for everyone? Why were they like this?

KEY INFORMATION FOR TEACHERS

Light entering our eyes gives us all sorts of information about the world, and we learn to interpret that at an early age. Two eyes placed at different points give us a wider field of vision. They also receive slightly different information, so our brains can interpret the different images to assist in judgements of distance and size. We call this stereoscopic vision.

Y1–Y2

Here are some different lights. What are they used for? What could you see with them?

Y3–Y4

Here are some torches you could buy. Find out which would be the best to have by your bed.

Y5–Y6

Find out how much light you need to read with. Will a small bulb be enough? Compare what you can see using some other light sources.

INVESTIGATING LIGHT SOURCES

Many activities with light such as these need to be done in a darkened room or a shady corner. Year 1 and 2 pupils can compare safe sources of light, such as battery-powered lanterns, spotlights and torches. Get them to explore which is brightest, how the light spreads out from each and what can be seen with them, for instance by shining each at a detailed picture. Children in years 3 and 4 should be encouraged to find simple ways of measuring the light from different sources, for example by seeing how many layers of tissue paper they have to put over a torch to block the light or by using it to read a piece of small print at increasing distances. Their results can be

tabulated and they can report back to the rest of the class orally or with pictures and writing. By years 5 and 6, children should be deciding how to measure or compare what they see (for example, by finding how far away they can read some print or by using a test chart (see Light 1)). If they can measure the brightness with a light meter or sensor, the investigation may be extended to quantify the relationship between light emitted and detail seen. They will need an effective blackout, but might devise their own on a small scale with a large box or a safe store cupboard. The following boxes suggest things teachers might say to children.

1 2 Questions and ideas	Tests, observations & measurements	Evidence and explanations
Which of these lights do you think is best for seeing things? What can you see with them?	Shine one at a picture. What can you see? Try another one – can you see exactly the same things?	Which is the best light to use for looking at the picture? Which would be best for lighting up the room?
3 4 Questions and ideas	Tests, observations & measurements	Evidence and explanations
Which is the brightest torch? How can you find out?	What can you do to measure how bright each one is? Are there any other ways to do it? Which do you think will work best?	Draw a table and pictures to show what you found out. How could you improve your test?
5 6 Questions and ideas	Tests, observations & measurements	Evidence and explanations
How well can you see with a 2.5 volt bulb? What difference do you think a brighter light would make? How can you test this?	How many different sorts of light will you test? What will you look at? How will you measure what you can see?	How does the amount of light affect what you see? Use a table or graph to help explain your findings.

KEY INFORMATION FOR TEACHERS

Light spreads out from a source. Because it travels so fast and reflects off many surfaces, light appears to happen instantaneously or just be all around. Children need to build up their understanding of how light travels and how reflected light from objects allows us to see the objects. The appearance of the object is affected by the amount of light reflected, so in dim light, the details and colours are harder to distinguish.

Y1–Y2

What shadows can you make on a sunny day?

Y3–Y4

Draw the shadow of your head on a piece of paper stuck on the wall. Work out how to make the shadow higher or lower.

Y5–Y6

Make shadows on a screen. Make the shadow get bigger and smaller. Find out how to make it twice as large.

INVESTIGATING SHADOWS

Year 1 and 2 children should be encouraged to play with their shadows. Extend their play into observations which lead them to predict what will happen ('If I do this, then my shadow will do this') and pursue their own questions ('How can I make my shadow do that?'). As they gain experience through shadow play indoors and out, they should notice patterns in their observations ('The shadow is always on the side away from the light'). By years 3 and 4, they can be asked to solve problems which require them to apply their observations, in this case how the shadow is raised by lowering the light source or by raising the object. Put the paper and the light and the pupil in a position so that only part of the shadow of their head falls onto the paper. They may

approach this by trial and error at first, but should be helped to change things one at a time and make sense of the findings. The relationship between the size of the shadow and the distance of the object from the screen is harder to grasp, but investigation of this should be within the grasp of year 5 and 6 pupils. They may need help to identify what to control and what to change, for example keeping the light fixed and just moving their hand, measuring the distance from hand to screen and the size of the shadow each time. A shadow puppet theatre is a good context for these investigations and gives children an opportunity to apply their learning. The following boxes suggest things teachers might say to children.

1 2 Questions and ideas	Tests, observations & measurements	Evidence and explanations
Where is your shadow? Does it always stay on that side? Can you make it go on the other side of you?	How can you make your shadow fatter? What will happen to your shadow if you bend down/stand sideways?	What makes your shadow? Why is it here? What makes it change shape?
3 4 Questions and ideas	Tests, observations & measurements	Evidence and explanations
How can you get the shadow of your head onto the paper so you can draw it?	Where will the shadow be if you stand up/kneel down? How can you make it fit the paper?	Draw pictures to show how the shadow is made. Use the pictures to help you explain why it is in that position.
5 6 Questions and ideas	Tests, observations & measurements	Evidence and explanations
What things could you change to make a bigger shadow on the screen? Test each one in turn.	What things are you measuring? Keep a table of your results and check them again.	Explain what happens to the shadow as you move the screen away from your hand.

KEY INFORMATION FOR TEACHERS

If light is blocked by an object, there is a shadow on the side opposite to the source of light. Light spreads out from a source in straight lines so the position and size of the shadow can be predicted. The shadow will get bigger as we increase the distance from the object to the surface on which the shadow falls.

Y1–Y2

Which things can you see yourself in? What do you look like?

Y3–Y4

Shine a torch at a target. Try to do it using a mirror. Shine the torch into the mirror and move the mirror till the light hits the target.

Y5–Y6

Stand a small figure in front of a mirror and look at its reflection. Investigate what happens if you use two mirrors, like this.

INVESTIGATING REFLECTIONS

Year 1 and 2 pupils should look at their reflection in a variety of surfaces, not just plane mirrors. They are likely to be struck most by the way they look funny in uneven and curved surfaces. Draw their attention to the similarities and differences in each case and to the contrast between good reflectors and poor ones. Large mirrors and ones with frames are useful at this stage. If glass mirrors are used cover the edges with tape if necessary and ensure there are no sharp points. Pupils in years 3 and 4 can begin investigating the way mirrors redirect a beam of light by tracing the path and drawing it. A torch with a sharp beam is needed; you may need to mask the torch with paper for this. By years 5 and 6, pupils should be able to record carefully what reflections they get using one and then two mirrors. At this stage, they should not only be able to make periscopes or kaleidoscopes but also use their growing understanding to predict what will happen as they adjust the angle between mirrors. The following boxes suggest things teachers might say to children.

1 2 **Questions and ideas**	**Tests, observations & measurements**	**Evidence and explanations**
Can you see yourself in these? Do you look different? What do you think you will look like in this spoon?	Look at yourself in the other side of the spoon. What do you look like? What's the difference?	Which of these things will give me a good reflection like a mirror? Which will make me look funny? What will I look like?
3 4 **Questions and ideas**	**Tests, observations & measurements**	**Evidence and explanations**
How can you use the mirror to reflect the light from the torch? Can you tell where it will go before you try it?	Make the light go where you want by moving the mirror. Find how to do it by keeping the mirror still and moving the torch.	Draw pictures to show what happens to the light when you shine it on the mirror.
5 6 **Questions and ideas**	**Tests, observations & measurements**	**Evidence and explanations**
How many reflections of the figure can you see? How many do you think there will be if you move the mirrors so the angle between them is smaller?	Stand the mirrors on a piece of paper, draw where they are and mark the figure. Note how many reflections there are. Do this again with the mirrors at different angles.	What happens to the number of reflections as you close the mirrors up together? It may help if you put your results in a table.

KEY INFORMATION FOR TEACHERS

Many surfaces will reflect light sufficiently and evenly enough to give a recognisable reflection. Rough, shiny surfaces reflect the light, but scatter it so the reflection is not recognisable. Mirrors reflect light evenly because they are smooth. A beam of light will reflect (bounce) off a mirror at the same angle as it strikes it. By moving the mirror to change the angle at which the beam strikes it, we can make the light go in a different direction. If it then strikes another mirror it is reflected again; by altering the angle between the mirrors, we can change the number of times it is reflected and therefore the number of reflections we can see.

Y1–Y2

Find out how many different sounds you can make with these things.

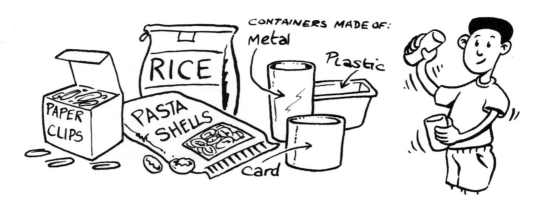

Y3–Y4

Make some simple musical instruments. What will you need to make a drum?

Y5–Y6

Find out how to make higher and lower notes with elastic bands or string.

INVESTIGATING SOUND PRODUCTION

Give year 1 and 2 children a small selection of materials and suggest how they could make their own instruments, such as shakers. Ask them to talk about how the sounds differ and what they think causes the differences. Get them to test their ideas, for example by changing the contents of a shaker. By years 3 and 4, pupils should be expected to predict and investigate the effects of different materials more systematically. With drums, they can change features – such as the size of the container they use, the sort of material they stretch across it, and how taut this is – one at a time to carry out fair tests. The volume and pitch of sound produced by drums might alter as a result. Children may confuse the terms 'high' and 'low' with the idea of loud or soft sounds. Older pupils should have the skills to plan their own investigations into how pitch changes as they tighten a vibrating string or elastic band. They need to identify and control other things which affect the pitch: the length and mass of the string or band. The following boxes suggest things teachers might say to children.

1 2 Questions and ideas	Tests, observations & measurements	Evidence and explanations
What sounds can you make with these? What will you put in your shaker?	Do these two shakers sound the same? How are they different?	What did you do to change the sounds? What do you need to make one that sounds like mine?
3 4 Questions and ideas	Tests, observations & measurements	Evidence and explanations
Which of these containers do you think will make the loudest drum? Why do you think this one will?	What else can you change on your drum to make a different sound? Test one at a time.	List the things which affect the sound a drum makes. What differences do they make?
5 6 Questions and ideas	Tests, observations & measurements	Evidence and explanations
Plan a test to find out how tightening strings (or elastic bands) changes the sound they make. What things will you need to keep the same each time?	What else could you change to make higher or lower notes?	What have you found affects the pitch of a string (or band) when you twang it? Make an elastic band instrument to play a tune.

KEY INFORMATION FOR TEACHERS

Sounds are made when something vibrates. Banging, shaking, scraping, plucking strings and blowing through holes or over the top of pipes all cause vibrations in the air around. Bigger vibrations, with a greater amplitude, make louder sounds. Faster vibrations, with a greater frequency, make higher-pitched sounds. Higher sounds come from shorter columns of air in wind instruments, and if we blow across the top of bottles, the note can be made higher by adding more water to shorten the column of air above it. Elastic bands or strings produce higher notes as they are tightened, but there are other things which affect the pitch, such as the length and mass of the bands or string.

Y1–Y2

Listen carefully. How many different sounds can you hear? Cover your ears and listen again. How many can you hear now?

Y3–Y4

Choose materials to make yourself some earmuffs that will keep sounds out. (Remember never to put things into your ears.)

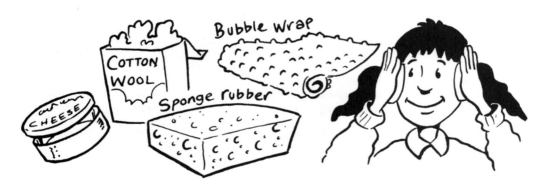

Y5–Y6

Plan a test to find out how well different materials will cut down noise.

INVESTIGATING SOUND INSULATION

Children in years 1 and 2 can explore the effects of putting their hands over their ears, wearing hats or scarves. Talk about how things sound quieter and different. Draw attention also to the times when they need to hear clearly, for instance when listening out for traffic. This is an opportunity to emphasise the importance of avoiding damage to ears through poking them and from loud sounds. Pupils in years 3 and 4 can make simple earmuffs to insulate against noise and appreciate the need for fair tests to compare different designs. Provide small containers for earpieces, a variety of materials for filling, and help them plan controlled investigations into the effect of different materials. Get them to use a standard sound, such as a buzzer or ticking clock, at increasing distances until it is inaudible. By years 5 and 6, pupils should begin to plan and conduct their own experiments to test the insulating properties of different materials, for instance by placing a source of sound, such as a bleeper or tape recorder, in a box filled with the insulating materials under test. They may need help in devising ways of measuring the sound, which could be done using a sound meter, a tape recorder which has a microphone and sound level indicator, or a sensor connected to the computer. The following boxes suggest things teachers might say to children.

1 2 Questions and ideas	Tests, observations & measurements	Evidence and explanations
How many sounds can you hear? Do you think you will still be able to hear them all if you put your hands over your ears?	Which sounds disappeared when you covered your ears? Find out which makes the world sound quieter – a scarf or hands over your ears.	How do sounds change when you cover your ears? Are they just quieter, or do they sound different?
3 4 Questions and ideas	Tests, observations & measurements	Evidence and explanations
Which materials do you think will be good for keeping sounds out?	How can you compare the different earmuffs to see which material works best?	Why do you think these are the best earmuffs? Why do you say that?
5 6 Questions and ideas	Tests, observations & measurements	Evidence and explanations
How well do you think each of these materials will cut down noise? Put them in order from best sound insulator to worst. Why will this one will be the best?	What will you do to measure the noise each time? Are you going to record your results in a table or a graph?	Did the materials work as you expected? Did the other groups get the same results as you? Where are insulators used to reduce noise?

KEY INFORMATION FOR TEACHERS

Some materials do not carry sound as well as others; they absorb sounds, so they are good sound insulators. The quality of sound is also affected by the materials it passes through, so it may sound different as well as quieter. Loudness is measured in decibels (dB). Listening to loud sounds (90 dB or more) can damage your hearing.

Y1–Y2

Listen to someone speak through these things. (Don't poke things into your ears.)

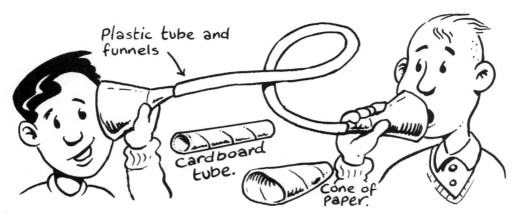

Plastic tube and funnels

cardboard tube.

Cone of paper.

Y3–Y4

Make a string telephone. Try different sorts of string to find out which works best.

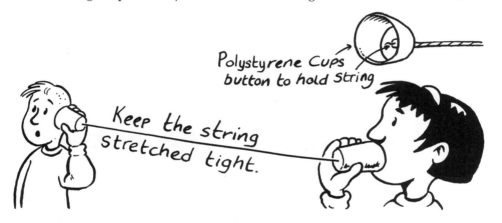

Polystyrene cups
button to hold string

Keep the string stretched tight.

Y5–Y6

Make a string telephone and try it out. List the things that you could change to make it work better. Plan a test to find out how one of those things does affect the telephone.

WE ARE CHANGING
size of cups.
WE ARE KEEPING THESE THE SAME.
Type of string.
Length of string.

INVESTIGATING HOW SOUND TRAVELS

Children in years 1 and 2 play language games where they have to identify sounds or repeat phrases, such as Chinese whispers. These can lead into activities such as the ones shown; they may need help and practice to send and hear the message. Play telephones made with tubing, cardboard tubes and paper cones can be compared to see which helps them hear voices best. They can be used as a stethoscope to listen for quiet sounds, like a heartbeat or ticking clock. All the activities in this section require a quiet setting. String telephones also need room to stretch out a long string safely. Making and testing them can be done with pupils of all ages, but around years 3 and 4 it is a good way to

develop more controlled investigations. Begin with only one key variable to change – for example, a few contrasting types of string, ranging from fine dental floss to thick wool – and keep other things, such as the distance and the containers, constant. The task for years 5 and 6 can be left very open to challenge able pupils, or more guidance can be given, for example by helping them to identify and list variables to control and test one at a time (such as shape and size of container, how the string is connected). Measurement is possible if they have a sound meter or a sensor connected to a computer. The following boxes suggest things teachers might say to children.

1 2 Questions and ideas	Tests, observations & measurements	Evidence and explanations
Do you think you will hear me through this? Will you hear me if I whisper?	What else could we use to listen through? Which is best for hearing really quiet sounds?	Which worked best? Why do you think it was this one?
3 4 Questions and ideas	Tests, observations & measurements	Evidence and explanations
Which string do you think will make the best telephone? Why? Does it have to be tight to work?	How will you test your idea? How will you decide which string is best?	What did you find out? Why do you think that string worked best? What else might you change to make a better telephone?
5 6 Questions and ideas	Tests, observations & measurements	Evidence and explanations
Have you made string telephones before? What things do you think affect how well they work? Make a list.	Which thing on your list are you testing first? What other things do you have to keep the same? How many tests will you need to do?	Put your results in a table and write a report to explain what you found out.

KEY INFORMATION FOR TEACHERS

Only some of the sound from a source reaches our ears. Tubes and funnels help us hear because the sound is reflected inside the tube and also because other sounds can be excluded. Speaking into the mouthpiece of a string telephone sets up vibrations which are carried along the string, if it is taut.

Y1–Y2

Draw round some shadows on the playground. Go back to them later.

Y3–Y4

Stand in one position in the classroom. Point to the position of the sun. Ask a friend to put a piece of paper on the window so it partly covers the sun.

Y5–Y6

Stand a pencil or straw in some plasticine on a sunny windowsill. Draw round its shadow every hour. Do this every month and put a date on each diagram.

INVESTIGATING THE SUN'S APPARENT MOVEMENT

In the year 1 and 2 activity, the children could record their observations in two drawings. Use different coloured chalk for the two different times. If possible, avoid doing the drawings either side of midday as the two shadows may have similar lengths. In the year 3 and 4 activity, the children should be warned against looking directly at the sun. Write the time of each observation on the paper. Shadow clocks can be made inside or outside, depending on local conditions. If you are using a cane or long stick, put a plastic cup or cork on the end to avoid poked eyes. The independent variables in these observations are the time of day, the time of year and the length of the object being used as a shadow stick. All these influence the dependent variable, which is the length of the shadow. The following boxes suggest things teachers might say.

1 2 Questions and ideas	Tests, observations & measurements	Evidence and explanations
Do you think the shadow will be the same when we come back later?	Try drawing round several things with different shapes and sizes. Have the shadows got longer or shorter? How do you know?	Why do you think the shadow moved?

3 4 Questions and ideas	Tests, observations & measurements	Evidence and explanations
In which direction is the sun during the morning break? Why do you think it has changed by the afternoon?	Do you think the pieces of paper would be stuck on the window in exactly the same place if you stood somewhere else in this room? Try it tomorrow, if it is sunny.	Draw a diagram showing where the paper was stuck on the window. When was the sun at its highest? When was it low in the sky? Why did it change position?

5 6 Questions and ideas	Tests, observations & measurements	Evidence and explanations
At which time of day would you expect the shadows to be shortest? Why do you think this is? In which directions do you expect the shadows to point at different times of the day?	Use several different size sticks. Draw round the shadows made by each stick at the same times of the day. Do they all show the same pattern of results? Use a magnetic compass to work out the direction in which the shadows point at noon each day.	Look at the shadow pictures you made last month. What differences do you notice? What similarities are there? Write some instructions for someone planning to make a shadow clock in their garden.

KEY INFORMATION FOR TEACHERS

The apparent motion of the sun across the sky is caused by the daily rotation of the Earth on its axis. If you look at the Earth from above the north pole, it rotates in an anticlockwise direction. This causes the sun to move from right to left across the sky, rising in the east and setting in the west. The length of the shadows cast by the sun changes as it gets higher and lower in the sky. At midsummer, the shadows at noon are relatively short and on midwinter's day they are much longer. However, both shadows point in the same direction. At no time is the sun directly overhead in England – it always shines from the south. On midsummer's day, the sun is directly overhead at the Tropic of Cancer, and it is overhead at the Tropic of Capricorn on midwinter's day.

Y1–Y2

Turn the globe so that part of it is in the shadow and part is in the light from the table lamp.

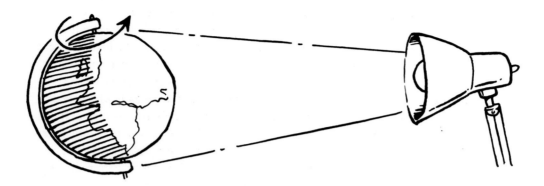

Y3–Y4

Shine a light at the globe. Stand a tiny figure on the globe on your home country. Turn the globe slowly. Stop it when you think the figure would have breakfast. What do you notice about its shadow? Do the same at lunchtime for the figure. What do you notice about its shadow now?

TURN GLOBE ANTICLOCKWISE.

Breakfast

Lunch time

Y5–Y6

Use a globe, some squared paper and strong light to explore why the equator gets stronger sunshine than the poles.

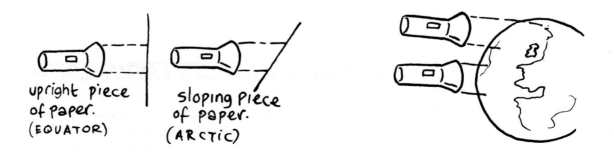

upright piece of paper. (EQUATOR)

sloping piece of paper. (ARCTIC)

INVESTIGATING A MODEL GLOBE

Put a small piece of card onto the globe to mark home for the children. Mark the countries where friends and relations live. Show the children the differences between the land and the sea. Tell them about the poles, equator and the tilted axis of the globe. Allow the children to explore the globe and turn it, noticing which part of the world is in the light whilst other parts are in the dark. For the year 3 and 4 activities, stick a small figure to the globe, ensuring that it just fits under the curved stand. It should cast a shadow as the globe is turned in a strong light. If possible, do this activity in a shaded room using a small globe and a powerful torch. Ask the children to notice that, as the earth is turned anticlockwise (if looking down on the north pole), the shadow of the stick moves. Set the eldest children the puzzle of trying to explain why the poles are colder than the equatorial areas. Small globes give better results than larger globes, especially when weak light sources are used. OHPs are the best light source, as they are safe and easy to use. Try, where possible, to do activities with globes and light sources in at least partial blackout. The following boxes suggest things teachers might say to children.

1 2 Questions and ideas	Tests, observations & measurements	Evidence and explanations
Where do you think the sun is during the night?	Turn the globe so that different parts of the world come into the sunlight.	Point to the parts of the world which come into the sunlight before us. Do you know the names of any of these places?
3 4 Questions and ideas	Tests, observations & measurements	Evidence and explanations
What do you think will happen to the shadow made by the figure as the globe turns?	Think of as many ways as possible to make the shadow of the figure get longer and shorter.	Turn the globe and show me the place where the shadow is very short. Why is it so short there? When is the figure's shadow long?
5 6 Questions and ideas	Tests, observations & measurements	Evidence and explanations
On which part of the globe do you think the torch's beam will be most concentrated. Suggest reasons why this is.	Point the torch beam directly at some squared paper. How many squares does it cover? Lean the paper over and count the number of squares it is spread over.	Explain why the sun's rays are so spread out at the poles and so concentrated at the tropics. Draw diagrams showing sunlight hitting the equator and polar areas.

KEY INFORMATION FOR TEACHERS

The shadow cast by the figure is long at dawn and evening and short at noon. If the figure is placed on Britain, it will always point in a northerly direction. The figure's shadow can be lengthened by arranging the globe so the northern hemisphere is away from the light (winter). In this position there is a relatively long shadow even at noon. The torch's light is spread out considerably when shone at an angle, and this mimics the way that the sun's rays are spread out in the northern hemisphere in winter and have little warming effect. At the equator, in contrast, the sun is nearly overhead and the rays are not spread out.

Planning for Progression through the School

This section of the book will help whole schools plan more effectively for progression in scientific investigations. The science co-ordinator and the head teacher can work together to set up the conditions needed for a school to operate an effective work scheme for science. Once this is in place, effective classroom science with progression from year to year becomes possible.

This section of the book outlines some of the strategies which have helped move schools forward. The advice is largely aimed at science co-ordinators, teachers with an interest in curriculum planning and head teachers. The following sequence will provide a useful checklist for action when planning for progression.

Review the present position.

↓

Prepare a school action plan for science.

↓

Increase staff awareness of progression.

↓

Increase staff confidence about science.

↓

Write a school science scheme.

↓

Draw up detailed guidance for progression.

TWELVE

Review the present position

The first task is to evaluate how far you feel your school has got in implementing a sound approach to scientific investigations. One school, whose approach is detailed towards the end of this section, embarked on a thorough review of their complete curriculum. They examined the balance between the different subjects and the topics they taught; these were subsequently changed as a result of their analysis.

You could, however, focus more narrowly on the science. With a colleague, use the following sheet (figure 3.1) to structure your evaluation of science in your school. Tell other colleagues about your perceptions or ask all the teachers to do the task in pairs during a staff meeting. You will probably find the process of comparing different perceptions to be productive.

MARK THE POSITION YOU THINK YOUR SCHOOL AND COLLEAGUES HAVE REACHED.

VERY FEW TEACHERS UNDERSTAND THE STATEMENTS OF ATTAINMENT FOR SCIENCE.
| 1 | 2 | 3 | 4 | 5 |
WE ALL FULLY GRASP THE IMPLICATIONS OF THE STATEMENTS OF ATTAINMENT.

THERE IS NOT MUCH SCIENTIFIC INVESTIGATION BEING DONE IN OUR SCHOOL.
| 1 | 2 | 3 | 4 | 5 |
ALL PUPILS ENGAGE IN INVESTIGATIONS.

OUR SCHEME OF WORK IS UNHELPFUL IN PLANNING FOR COVERAGE OF NATIONAL CURRICULUM SUBJECTS.
| 1 | 2 | 3 | 4 | 5 |
WE HAVE A USEFUL SCHEME OF WORK FOR SCIENCE AND ALL OTHER AREAS OF THE CURRICULUM.

THERE IS A VERY PATCHY PROVISION OF SCIENTIFIC EXPERIENCES.
| 1 | 2 | 3 | 4 | 5 |
THERE IS A BALANCED PROGRAMME COVERING ALL ASPECTS OF SCIENCE.

A LIMITED NUMBER OF SCIENCE SKILLS ARE TAUGHT.
| 1 | 2 | 3 | 4 | 5 |
AT1 AND THE OTHER ATs ARE TAUGHT IN HARMONY.

THE OLDER CHILDREN WORK AT A SIMILAR LEVEL TO THE YOUNGER ONES.
| 1 | 2 | 3 | 4 | 5 |
THERE IS A PROGRESSION OF SKILLS AND IDEAS.

WE HAVE VERY FEW RESOURCES.
| 1 | 2 | 3 | 4 | 5 |
WE HAVE EVERYTHING WE NEED.

STAFF HAVE DIFFICULTY IN ASSESSING SCIENCE.
| 1 | 2 | 3 | 4 | 5 |
SATs AND TEACHER ASSESSMENT PLAY A VITAL ROLE IN OUR PLANNING FOR SCIENCE.

Figure 3.1   Evaluate the present position of science

THIRTEEN

Prepare a school action plan for science

Once you have begun to clarify the position of the school and to draw up lists of priorities, it is time to write an action plan. To help you to draw up your plan, consider the following points.

- How will you ensure the provision and maintenance of resources?
- How will colleagues be helped to find equipment?
- How will you involve the head teacher in developing science?
- Where will you put most of your energy, with the reluctant teachers or the enthusiastic ones?
- Does the present policy for science need rewriting?
- What areas of science knowledge can you help colleagues to understand?

- What will you tackle as your main priorities and what can wait?
- What are your short-term objectives (this year)?
- What are your long-term objectives (three years)?
- How will you monitor progress in the development of science?

Here is the action plan prepared by Brenda Orr, the science co-ordinator at Thorne Green Top First School, Doncaster. The school covers years 1 to 4. Notice that Brenda suggests a time scale and builds in evaluation from the start. This plan was shown to the head teacher and agreed as a plan for the school.

ACTION PLAN TARGETS

1 Provide adequate resources.
2 Write a school policy.
3 Ensure progression of skills from reception to year 4.
4 Integrate skills and knowledge into planning. Use assessment information.

SHORT-TERM ACTION

Aims

To raise awareness of the importance of scientific investigations.
To develop continuity and progression throughout the school.

TIME	ACTION	RESOURCES	EVALUATION
June–July	Make an inventory of both class and central resources.	Files.	Are the resources being used?
	Order new resources.	Finance.	
	Organise storage.		
Lunchtimes	Workshops for staff on investigations.	DFE course material and published resources.	Staff feedback on the usefulness of the workshops.
July	Visit local college for discussions about best way to plan, record and assess AT1.	Cover for science co-ordinator.	Review of staff planning sheets by science co-ordinator.
September	Staff to review present science policy.	Present policy.	Have the staff felt confident enough to express their views?
	Consider different published resources for purchase.	Variety of published materials. Finance.	Was there enough to choose from?
October	Continue investigation workshops.	DFE course material.	Is there more investigation taking place in classrooms? Is it reflected in staff planning sheets?

MID-TERM ACTION

Aim

To produce a scheme of work which gives guidance on how skills and concepts are to be developed.

TIME	ACTION	RESOURCES	EVALUATION
November	Help teachers to identify the possibilities for practical activity in their science theme or topic.	A range of science activities.	Is there a balance for the activities planned for next term?
Lunchtimes	Form small working party to review previous scheme of work and to begin planning new one. Devise some detailed plans for progression in teaching concepts.	Previous scheme of work. LEA document. DFE course material.	What other schemes of work need improving?
January–March	Co-ordinator to work alongside colleagues in class.	Cover for co-ordinator.	Feedback from colleagues.
	Rewrite science policy to include changes suggested by staff.	Teachers comments on draft policy.	Is the policy accessible and understandable to teachers, supply teachers and governors?
After school	Review assessment policy.	Colleagues responsible for other curriculum areas.	Are the changes suggested welcomed by colleagues?

LONG-TERM ACTION

Aims
To set up a science management team.
To involve parents.

TIME	ACTION	RESOURCES	EVALUATION
April–June	Continue sorting and filing resources.	Finance.	Are the resources now adequate?
	Plan for other staff to attend INSET courses.	Information about INSET opportunities.	Have enough staff received training to form a management team?
July	Meet with head teacher to review the previous action. List our new priorities.	Teachers planning and recording sheets.	How many of our objectives and aims have we achieved?
July	Invitation to KS1 and KS2 parents to do science activities in the hall.	Science equipment. Cover for co-ordination.	Did parents show interest? Is it worth repeating?
September	Start a science club.	Science equipment, energy and enthusiasm.	Are the children enjoying the club?

FOURTEEN

Increase staff awareness of progression

In many schools, teachers work in isolation from each other for most of the time. This means there are usually few opportunities to see scientific investigations being done by different age groups. Here are two ways which have been successful.

A SCHOOL SCIENCE WEEK

One of the most potent ways of making staff aware of the opportunities for progression is to undertake a school science week on a common theme. This need not be very ambitious in the first instance, and, where possible, you should try to avoid making extra work for the staff. One of the topics in section two of this book might provide a central organising theme for the science week. Forces or Electricity would probably be challenging, whilst Growth might suit less confident members of staff.

Before starting the detailed planning, roughly map out the sorts of differences in investigations you would expect from different age groups. A very rough-and-ready version might be along the following lines:

Infants (Years 1 and 2):	Observe simple changes and events. Ask questions and try out ideas.
Lower juniors (Years 3 and 4):	Plan simple tests and carry them out. Use evidence to support ideas.
Upper juniors (Years 5 and 6):	Plan tests based on scientific ideas suggesting the sorts of things they expect to find out.

In addition to detailing types of investigations they would expect, teachers could map out the scientific ideas the children will learn and investigate. For instance, if you looked at electricity:

Infants (Years 1 and 2):	Very simple circuits.
Lower juniors (Years 3 and 4):	Conduction of electricity.
Upper juniors (Years 5 and 6):	The effects of different bulbs and batteries in circuits.

These activities are detailed in section two on pages 82–85 (which shows a progression in terms of investigations) and in this section of the book on pages 129–131 (which demonstrates progression in the scientific ideas).

Once the scientific investigations have taken

place in each year, the resulting work could be placed on desks around a room. Unless you have staff who are keen to mount a school-wide exhibition of work for science, try to avoid the temptation, especially in the early stages, to make it into a display, where some less-confident staff may feel threatened.

Encourage colleagues to study the work from different age groups and to talk about their perceptions of the level of the work and look for instances of progression, overlap and repetition. The experience of seeing progression, or perhaps lack of it, in a concrete form is a very powerful aid to discussion.

WORKING ALONGSIDE COLLEAGUES

Another powerful strategy for raising awareness about what is happening in science throughout the school is to arrange for teachers to plan and work alongside colleagues in different year groups. The active participation of the head teacher will be essential.

The Initiative in Primary Science: an Evaluation (IPSE) Report (ASE, 1987) found that lasting beneficial change took place when science co-ordinators worked alongside colleagues. This was particularly pronounced when the class teacher retained overall responsibility for the work. It is important to bear in mind that a lasting improvement in practice depends on increasing teacher's confidence.

FIFTEEN

Increase staff confidence about science

There are two areas where staff will probably need help:

- planning and providing resources for science activities;

- scientific knowledge and planning for investigations.

PLANNING AND PROVIDING RESOURCES FOR SCIENCE ACTIVITIES

Where possible, the science co-ordinator should work alongside colleagues as they plan their science work. This could be at the level of planning out the science for half a term or simply the next lesson. This assistance will help with the immediate need to plan and will also give the science co-ordinator opportunity to point out where there are possibilities for progression.

Often the major block to carrying out science is the lack, or perceived lack, of resources. The science co-ordinator should find ways of telling colleagues what is available. A list of all the science equipment and publications held in the school is invaluable.

SCIENCE KNOWLEDGE AND PLANNING FOR INVESTIGATIONS

One way in which to approach this detailed planning is for the science co-ordinator to offer informal sessions at lunchtime or after school where staff can do activities based on material in this book or in science schemes. In *Primary Science Investigations*, Johnsey also suggests a useful range of activities related to Sc1.

If you are fortunate enough to get a half day's INSET for staff development in science, you might consider focusing on Sc1. You may want to use the following structure. Naturally you will need to be selective if you have only a short time available.

Beforehand the science co-ordinator will need to prepare the following materials:

- copies of Attainment Target 1 from Science in the National Curriculum;
- for each group: three or four balls (rubber ball, airflow ball, sponge ball, tennis ball), a cardboard slope, some wooden blocks, large sheets of paper and writing materials, metre

rules, a room with several different floor surfaces;

- one example (a different one for each group) of a year 3 and 4 investigation from this book.

Remind colleagues that throughout they should work at their own level.

9.00   Explain structure of the day.
Discuss Attainment Target 1 of Science (Sc1) in the National Curriculum.
Science co-ordinator to clarify, if possible, any points raised.

9.15   Ask teachers to get into mixed age groups of three or four.
Which ball rolls down the slope furthest? Predict first.
Record your results in at least two different ways.
Roll the balls down the slope then onto a level surface.
How far does each roll?
Plan, then carry out an investigation into how far they will roll when the level surface is covered with different surfaces like lino, corrugated card, wooden desktop.
Once the activity has been done, ask the teachers to suggest differences in the way this investigation could be approached three stages (for example, year 2, year 4 and year 6).

10.00   Look at the bouncing balls progression on page 66.
Work through the three suggested activities.
All staff work on the problems and opportunities associated with having both the ball and the surface a variable in the year 5 and 6 example.

10.30–10.45 BREAK

10.45   Give each group of three or four teachers a different year 3 and 4 investigation from section two of this book. Simply copy the relevant section from the left hand side of several spreads. Ask them to discuss it, list equipment needed, list the science skills they could easily develop from the activity. They should then specify one similar year 1 and 2 activity and one similar year 5 and 6 activity.
Once they have completed the task, give them the full double-page spread. Ask each group to compare their ideas to the ones suggested by the authors.

11.30   Get together to share ideas as a whole staff.
Discuss the differences between investigations at the three stages.

12.00–1.00 LUNCH

If you have more than a half day, consider setting out sets of equipment and some cards or books aimed at children. The themes could be:

- investigating batteries and bulbs;
- investigating magnets;
- investigating different types of paper.

SIXTEEN

Write a school science scheme

THE SCIENCE SUBJECT APPROACH

Schools are required to produce both a policy and a scheme of work for science. A policy is a short document which provides a broad statement of aims and approaches and reflects the philosophy of a school. It gives guidance to teachers, parents, inspectors and governors about the school's approach to specific issues in the teaching of science. An example of a policy can be found in *Science with Reason* (Atkinson, 1995).

In terms of ensuring progression, however, the school's scheme of work is an essential document. To avoid repetition, it is necessary to draw up a scheme which shows colleagues the areas which should be tackled in particular year groups. Your scheme must be short and easy to understand, because teachers will also have schemes of work for all others areas of the curriculum in addition to science. If the scheme is complex, it will be ignored because of the pressure of work. Teachers have little time to spend reading and digesting long documents. You must also avoid being overly prescriptive, since this will stifle the creativity of the best teachers.

Below is a suggestion for a very bare framework for a scheme of work in science. We have avoided linking the area of science to topics (such as Transport or The seasons) for three reasons.

- Topics may not be the most appropriate way to plan for science in every case.
- Individual teachers should have as much responsibility for their own planning as possible and so should build their own curriculum using the elements suggested for their year group.
- Where the topic approach is used, there are local considerations which will mean that a topic which is ideal in one place is inappropriate in another.

The scheme below is the result of an analysis of the programmes of study which are the basis of deciding what to teach. It is structured on a two-year programme so that, in general, children will not be taught about the same area of science two years in succession. This is helpful when dealing with mixed-age classes, although it does not entirely solve the problems this can entail.

Each year of the scheme starts with a short sentence about the type of investigations which should be going on in an average class of that age. Naturally, you and your colleagues may want to alter the detail of this, but experience shows that teachers respond positively to pithy benchmark statements in straightforward language.

Key Stage 1 (years 1 and 2) Possible allocation of science programmes of study

Year 1	Year 2
Scientific investigation, including observation, and first hand experience of a variety of materials and events.	Scientific investigation, including simple testing of materials and events. Increasing use of measurement. Making simple records of investigations.
Human growth and development Senses Keeping healthy Sounds Light Weather	Plants and animals Similarities and differences Natural and manufactured materials Hot and cold Magnets Forces: floating and sinking, gravity Electricity

Key Stage 2a (years 3 and 4) Possible allocation of science programmes of study

Year 3	Year 4
Scientific investigation, including making fair tests, using standard measurements and using results to come to conclusions.	Scientific investigation, including making predictions, fair testing. See the need, to be accurate and repeat readings to check results.
Human organs and systems Plant parts and life cycles Soils Properties of materials Floating and sinking Earth and seasons Light and shadows	A habitat near school The water cycles Electric circuits Changing materials Magnets Energy sources and burning Sound and echoes

Key Stage 2b (years 5 and 6) Possible allocation of science programmes of study

Year 5	Year 6
Scientific investigation, including making predictions with reasons for their prediction. Being able to recognise some of the factors that may affect the result of an experiment.	Scientific investigation, including seeking the answers to questions raised by themselves. Designing their own tests where they recognise the main factors which might affect the results. Routinely repeating measurements to check the validity of their results.
Human reproduction and health Plants and food chains Rocks Separating materials Forces, air resistance and force diagrams Earth and planets Colour, light and sight	Contrasting habitats and adaptations to environment Using keys and classification Variety of electric circuits and components Solids, liquids and gases Forces, friction and falling Energy storage and transfer Sound and sound-proofing

THE TOPIC APPROACH TO A SCIENCE SCHEME: ONE SCHOOL'S EXPERIENCE

This section was written by Sue Tambar with Allan Denford, who, at the time of writing, both taught at Pipworth Junior School, Sheffield. It shows how they took the above suggestions for the allocation of science programmes of study and worked them into topics for their school. They felt that a topic approach was the best way to encourage staff to do more science because:

- staff are used to working in topics;
- staff want an integrated approach to the curriculum.

Introduction

Before undertaking the review of my school's scheme of work for science, I attended a DfE twenty day science course, which broadened my own understanding of science and gave me confidence to help my colleagues with some of the problems they encountered when planning and teaching science. Prior to this, I had a limited science background, only having studied chemistry and biology to O level. I later did a short science course as part of my post-graduate teaching certificate.

I was recently appointed science co-ordinator at Pipworth Junior School, an inner-city school serving a large housing estate. There are approximately sixty children in each year group, giving a total population of 240 children. Each year group shares a teaching base and operates as a team. Planning and teaching together is an accepted way of working in the school.

Topics have formed the basis of planning for some time, and each year group uses an agreed set of topics. These were planned to ensure that, over four years, a child experienced a variety of topics with few repetitions. The established staff know their topics well, and there are adequate teaching resources.

I decided to review the topics taught in the school to check whether:

- all the important areas of science were covered by the topics;
- scientific areas were taught twice in key stage 2, with a reasonable intervening period, to allow for progression and continuity.

I involved the head teacher and the curriculum co-ordinator (Allan Denford). All of us felt that to look at science in isolation would not be helpful, as it should be seen as an integral part of all topics. This meant that what had

PLEASE WRITE IN THE NAME OF THE TOPIC YOU COVER. LIST THE ACTIVITIES YOU DO UNDER EACH HEADING. IF APPROPRIATE PLEASE INCLUDE THE RELEVANT NATIONAL CURRICULUM ATTAINMENT TARGET.

TOPIC :	TIME OF YEAR & LENGTH
ENGLISH	
MATHS	
SCIENCE	
HISTORY	
GEOGRAPHY	
TECHNOLOGY	
ARTS, MUSIC, PE, HEALTH	
RE, PERSONAL/SOCIAL, ENVIRONMENTAL	

Figure 3.2 Topic chart

started out as a check on the coverage of science was going to affect all aspects of our teaching. I had to ensure that my findings were based on accurate information and that all the staff were involved from the start.

Finding out about the present situation

At the next staff meeting, there was a brief discussion; staff were told about the project and asked to fill in two topic review sheets to supply up-to-date information about the topics they used

to structure their teaching. Everyone agreed that it was important that our planning should start by understanding the present position and that we should build from there.

Each member of staff filled in a separate topic chart showing the elements of each of the topics taught (figure 3.2). All the information was then collated to give a picture for the whole school. The results are shown in the existing School Topic Plan (figure 3.3). The information from the topic charts also enabled us to compile a School Curriculum Chart (figure 3.4).

	TERM 1			TERM 2		TERM 3		
YEAR 3	AUTUMN	ROCKS	DINOSAURS	WINTER	SPACE	HOUSES AND HOMES		
YEAR 4	WOOD AND TREES			POLICE	HEALTH	SEASIDE	CASTLES	
YEAR 5	MYSELF		FOOTBALL	TOYS	TUDORS & STUARTS	MY BODY	EARTH CARE	
YEAR 6	HABITATS	VICTORIAN	COMMUNICATION		CONSERVATION			

Figure 3.3 Existing school topic plan

BLANK SQUARE: NOT INCLUDED.   ✔ SMALL ELEMENT OF THE TOPIC.

✔✔ SUBSTANTIAL ELEMENT.   ✔✔✔ CENTRAL TO THE TOPIC.

TOPIC	ENG	MATH	SCI	TECH	GEOG	HIST	ART	MUS	P E	R E	PERS
ROCKS	✔✔		✔	✔	✔✔	✔✔	✔✔				
DINO-SAURS	✔✔		✔	✔		✔	✔				
AUTUMN	✔✔		✔		✔		✔				
ROMANS	✔			✔	✔	✔✔✔	✔				✔
WEATHER	✔✔	✔	✔✔	✔	✔✔		✔✔				
SPACE	✔✔		✔✔	✔✔				✔			✔
HOUSES	✔✔	✔	✔✔	✔✔	✔✔	✔✔	✔✔				✔✔

Figure 3.4 School curriculum chart

When I looked at this chart, it was clear that I needed more information regarding the coverage of science. In particular, I was concerned to check whether some areas of science were omitted whilst others were repeated too many times. I used the list of possible allocation of the science programmes of study (see pages 122–123) and checked how often each was taught through the school. It was clear, once I had made the chart (figure 3.5), that there were many omissions. There were also several instances where the same aspect of science was repeated in every school year.

ASPECT OF SCIENCE	Y3	Y4	Y5	Y6
PLANT AND ANIMAL REPRODUCTION	✪			✪
ORGANS OF THE HUMAN BODY			✪	
HEALTH			✪	
ROTTING AND DECAY		✪	✪	✪
SIMPLE STRUCTURES				
AND SO ON.........				

✪ INDICATES THAT THIS ASPECT IS TAUGHT IN THAT YEAR.

Figure 3.5   Section of chart showing how many times areas of science were taught under the old scheme

New scheme of work

We thus set about drawing up a new set of topics which would assist staff to cover more of the science programmes of study. It was felt that it was important to retain as many of the existing topics as possible. We tried to ensure that year 3 topics were teamed with those in year 5. Similarly, year 4 and year 6 topics were teamed. Figure 3.6 shows a list of proposed topics. In general, the staff agree that these topic titles will help them plan a more logical and systematic treatment of science. The process of arriving at these titles has been time consuming, but because we have tried to involve everyone at each stage, there is a feeling of sharing and being part of changing an important aspect of the whole school's curriculum.

COMMENTARY

This account by Sue and Allan represents part of the continuing process of curriculum development, of which science is a major part. At the time of writing, Sue and Allan had presented their ideas for the new topic arrangement to the staff, and their efforts have, for the most part, been positively welcomed.

Success is not guaranteed, but they have several things in their favour. They have:

- a supportive head teacher;
- evolved their new plans for progression from an existing scheme;
- avoided throwing away all the hard work and planning of the past;
- made strenuous attempts to carry the staff with them.

Staff will need to see benefits quite quickly if they are to adopt the new approach whole-

YEAR 3	YEAR 5
WATER	WEATHER
MYSELF	BODY PROJECT
UNDERGROUND	LOCAL GARDEN STUDY
HOUSES AND HOMES	TOYS AND GAMES
SUN AND SEASONS	EARTH AND SPACE
INVADERS	TUDORS AND STUARTS
YEAR 4	**YEAR 6**
PEOPLE WHO HELP US	THE COMMUNITY
COLOUR AND SOUND	SENSES
TRANSPORT	COMMUNICATIONS
GROWING (plants and animals)	HABITATS
EXPLORERS	VICTORIANS
MINIBEASTS	ENERGY

Figure 3.6 List of proposed topics

heartedly. Teachers will want to know what advantages there are in the new scheme when they are being asked to abandon what has worked well for them over several years. All the staff at Pipworth, in common with almost all primary schools, may have to overcome the following problems:

- Resistance to change, brought on by too many alterations to working patterns over the past six years.
- Reversion to previous practice because of the time and energy spent resourcing and learning about the old set of topics.
- Insecurity, most likely to affect those who teach the older children. This is because they may feel they lack the knowledge to take older children further in ecology, for instance, when they have already been taught the basics of plant and animal relationships.
- Alienation, felt by some who feel that they are being told what to do by an inner core group. The need for small groups to press on with

changes to different aspects of the school curriculum is an inevitable result of the pressure on all teachers' time.
- Gap between the theory and practice of curriculum change. There might be many possibilities for science work within each topic, but, under pressure, science may simply be given lip service and no more.

Lastly, the teachers in this school have invested a large amount of time and energy in analysing their topic structure and then proposing an improvement. Has their time been well spent? There is a tacit understanding that English and maths are less reliant on a topic framework to give them context. This is shown by the fact that the central focus of a topic is rarely maths or English. Should science move towards this position? Science could be seen more as a separate subject which builds on previous experience rather needing to be given context from parallel experiences in other curriculum areas.

SEVENTEEN

Draw up detailed guidance for progression

Whether you choose to plan from topics, from science ideas or from a mixture of the two, most teachers will need help in deciding what knowledge to teach a particular age group. This advice should complement the published schemes. Appendix 1 is an example of the sort of guidelines you might find useful.

Appendix 1

Progression in teaching electricity

Key Stage 1 (years 1 and 2)

Main idea	Equipment	Notes and background
Electricity is dangerous.	Look at some mains equipment.	The message should be clear and unambiguous. Electricity from the mains is very dangerous. Do not play with plugs, wires, sockets or anything which is plugged into the mains.
Most batteries are safe.	Show, and let the children play with, safe, battery-operated toys.	Most batteries are safe, but do not use rechargeable batteries in any investigations. If they are short circuited, they get very hot.
You need a complete circuit to make a bulb light.	Two wires with clips already attached. Bulb in bulb holder. Cell in cell holder.	Let the children experiment and find out for themselves how to make a circuit. Electricity will only flow when there is a complete circuit. The only slight problem is that the children may short-circuit the battery, so don't use new batteries here.

Key Stage 2 (years 3 and 4)

Main idea	Equipment	Notes and background
One battery can light two bulbs.	One cell in a holder, two bulbs in holders, three wires.	Challenge the children to make both bulbs light. Wiring them in series makes the electricity pass through both bulbs. If both bulbs are identical, they will be equally bright. If they are slightly different, one bulb will glow more brightly than the other. Change the position of the bulbs and observe the effect on their brightness. The dim bulb will remain dim, no matter which position it is in.
Some materials conduct electricity.	A simple circuit made with three wires, one cell in holder, one bulb in holder. Metal, wood and plastic objects.	Make a gap between two wires in the circuit. Clip the sample of material between the wires and see if the bulb lights. All metals conduct electricity, but remember that some metals are coated in paint or varnish, which does not conduct electricity.
A switch can control electrical flow.	Soft board, two scraps of foil, drawing pins, a simple circuit made using three wires.	Clip the two pieces of wire to the scraps of foil. Hold the foil on the board using pins so that the circuit is made when the ends of the foil touch. Investigate how other very simple home-made and bought switches work. Make models which use simple circuits, switches and series circuits.
Electricity makes a motor turn.	One cell, one motor, two wires and clips.	When you reverse the connections to the cell, the motor spins in the opposite direction.

Key Stage 2 (years 5 and 6)

Main idea	Equipment	Notes and background
More cells give a higher voltage	One bulb, two or more cells in series.	Connect the cells positive to negative. Work out the voltage of this battery of cells – simply add their voltages. Notice that the bulb glows very brightly with high voltages. The filament will melt if the voltage is too high.
Drawing circuit diagrams.	Simple circuits.	The symbols for components are shown in many publications.
Other devices can be put into electrical circuits.	LEDs, 3 v battery. Motor Buzzer	Make a simple circuit with a 3 v battery and an LED. Make simple circuits with buzzers or motors. Make a Morse code signaller.
Open-ended investigations are possible for bright children, using electrical components.	LEDs, batteries, wires and clips, bulbs.	Does the LED work either way round? What happens who you put two LEDs in series? What happens when you put an LED in series with a bulb? Try to match the voltage of the battery to the number of LEDs you use.

Bibliography

These are the books which have been referred to in the text. There are a great many other readable books about primary science and primary science investigations.

Atkinson, S. (ed.) *Science with Reason*, Hodder Headline, London, 1995.

ASE *Be Safe*, ASE. Hatfield, (latest edition).

ASE *IPSE: Report*, ASE, Hatfield, 1987.

DFE, *Key Stages 1 and 2 of the National Curriculum*, HMSO. London, 1995.

Frost, R. *The IT in Primary Science Book*, ASE, Hatfield, 1993.

Goldsworthy, A. and Feasey, R. *Making Sense of Science Investigations*, ASE, Hatfield, 1994.

Harlen, W. *Primary Science: Taking the Plunge*, Heinemann, London, 1985.

Johnsey, R. *Primary Science Investigations*, Simon and Schuster, London, 1992.

NCC *Curriculum Guidance 10 – Teaching Science to Pupils with Special Educational Needs*, NCC, York, 1992.

NCET *IT's Primarily Science* [a series of leaflets on how computers can help Key Stage 2 science], NCC, Coventry, 1994.

Peacock, G. and Smith, R. *Teaching and Understanding Science*, Hodder Headline, London, 1992.